The Art of Whittling:
A Beginner's Guide to Woodcarving

Step-by-Step Projects and Techniques for Crafting Beautiful Wooden Objects by Hand

Copyright © 2023

All rights reserved. No part of this publication may be reproduced, stored in a retrieval system, or transmitted in any form or by any means, electronic, mechanical, photocopying, recording, scanning, or otherwise, without the prior written permission of the Publisher.

This book is dedicated to Larry Chambers, who taught me how to teach, and to my parents, who showed me how to build the life I want.

CONTENTS

INTRODUCTION

CHAPTER ONE: Whittling 101

CHAPTER TWO: Beginner Whittling Projects

- **Simple Butter Spreader**
- **S'mores Roasting Stick**
- **Whittled Toggles**
- **Whittled Tent Stake**
- **Magic Wand**
- **Hairpin**
- **Leaf Pendant**
- **Whittled Trees**
- **Simple Fishing Handline**

CHAPTER THREE: Skill-Building Projects

- **Whittled Egg**
- **Small Salt Bowl**
- **Woven-Knot Pendant**
- **Spiral Ornament**
- **Comfort Bird**
- **Salad Servers**

Perching Owl

Lidded Box

Whittled Whale

CHAPTER FOUR: Intermediate and Inspirational Projects

Whittled Spoon

Fox Figurine

Toy Bear

Garden Gnome

Chess Pieces

Wood Spirit

PATTERNS

RESOURCES

ACKNOWLEDGMENTS

INTRODUCTION

In this Book the author describes how she first got into whittling while on a camping trip, and how it became a peaceful and stress-relieving activity for her. She went on to work as a whittling teacher, and through her experience teaching, she developed an interest in communicating information in ways that make sense to the most people. The author believes that whittling is a great hobby that teaches patience and perseverance, and requires only a knife, a block of wood, and some safety knowledge. The book provides a foundation for tool and safety information, followed by a series of beginner projects that build upon each other. The projects in the book are designed to help readers learn and practice the fundamental techniques of whittling, and the book also contains more challenging projects for those who want to take their skills to the next level.

ONE

WHITTLING 101

This chapter will provide the foundational knowledge you'll need for the projects in the rest of this book, including where to get your knives and what qualities to look for in a good whittling knife. You'll also learn where to source your materials and which wood types are best for whittling. In addition to details on tools and materials, you'll be provided comprehensive information on whittling safety, knife techniques, sharpening, and finishing techniques. Whether you are an absolute beginner or have whittled before, the information in this chapter will make you feel confident and prepared to begin the projects in the subsequent chapters.

Welcome to the World of Whittling

In its simplest form, whittling is the process of removing wood with a knife to transform the wood into a decorative or functional object. Decorative projects include figures, pendants, and accessories. Functional projects include utensils for cooking and rustic projects for camping, such as tent stakes and a fishing handline. With a few hand tools, you can carve all the projects in this book, each from a single piece of wood.

    Whittling is a time-honored skill practiced around the world. Its emphasis on creativity and accessibility has stood the test of time. In modern times, whittling has become a widely popular hobby practiced by people internationally. Although it can appear to be a solitary hobby, there are many ways to turn it into a group activity. There are strong online communities of whittlers and yearly gatherings and festivals. Plenty of cities have whittling and hobby shops, and many have local clubs that meet regularly. Since whittling is such an easy craft to get into, you can even get a few friends involved and start a whittling group of your own.

    This book aims to teach you all the fundamental knowledge and skills you need to begin your whittling journey. Here, you will begin with a comprehensive informational foundation regarding tools, materials, accessories, and safety. The book then details the basic knife techniques integral to every whittling project. The projects in the chapters that follow have been carefully selected to offer many opportunities for practicing these core techniques. As the book progresses, the projects become more complex and require you to combine techniques in new and exciting ways. All the projects are beginner-friendly and don't require the use of power tools. With the foundation that this book provides, you will be able to take your whittling skills anywhere.

Whittling versus Carving

When you think of shaping wood with knives, two terms defining the process come to mind: whittling and carving. Though whittling and carving are technically the same, they have quite different applications in the world of woodworking. While whittling can be done on the go with just a few tools, carving often involves a workshop, vise, and dozens of specialized tools. Although the two words are used interchangeably in the projects, this book focuses overall on whittling for the following reasons:

FEWER TOOLS AND MATERIALS: If you are like me, it's easy to want to go all-out on a new hobby. However, beginning a hobby that requires an entire woodshop, workbench, and a series of specialized tools is much less realistic than picking up a nice whittling knife, some basswood blocks, and this book.

TAKE PROJECTS ON THE GO: You can bring whittling projects with you nearly anywhere. Just be sure to put the whittling tools in your checked luggage.

GREAT FOR RELAXATION: Whittling is a fun and relaxing hobby. The low barrier to entry frees you up to spend less time learning, measuring, and preparing and more time whittling fun projects.

Whittler's Kit

In addition to a good whittling knife, which we will cover in the next section, you will want a few other items in your whittling kit. The following items will help you accomplish the projects in this book. Most of them are relatively inexpensive. You might even have some in your house already!

CARVING GLOVES: Whether you are just starting out or do not want to risk an accidental hand injury, carving gloves are great to have in your whittling kit. Look for cut-resistant Kevlar gloves at the local hardware store. Some people believe that carving gloves can encourage bad technique because knife safety isn't as necessary when you wear them. Treat your gloves like a protective layer for accidental slips rather than an invincibility shield. After all: Great knights still wore armor.

DESIGN MATERIALS: These materials include a measuring tape and a pencil. I recommend getting an oil-based or a high-B artist pencil (4B and above) because it writes well on wood. A small measuring tape helps you mark guidelines on projects that do not require a pattern.

DETAIL CARVING CHISELS: Although whittling projects can technically be done with just a knife, a detail chisel or set of gouges (curved profile chisels) can allow you to add details to your project safely and effectively. Many palm gouges for details come in sets. Good brands to consider are Flexcut, Pfeil, and PowerGrip.

HAND SAW: A good hand saw is essential for preparing blanks, sawing wood handholds off smaller pieces after whittling, and harvesting wood in the wild. A nice folding saw with medium or fine teeth and a curved blade is a great all-purpose option. Good brands to look for include Silky and Fiskars.

STROP: Essential for sharpening, a strop is a piece of leather with a hard backing that holds stropping compound, a mildly abrasive paste. The strop is used to hone and polish your knife between sharpenings.

WHETSTONE: This sharpening tool is a *must* to keep your blades sharp and safe. A whetstone is a flat, abrasive stone that is used with liquid to sharpen your knife. The two main types are oilstones (used with oil) and water stones (used with water). There are many good two-grit water stones, such as Messermeister, on the market. You can make your own sharpening system by purchasing several different grits of high-grit machinist sandpaper and mounting them each on its own base of tempered glass or hardwood.

Know Your Knives

Your whittling knife will be your most important tool. Therefore, it's important to understand several characteristics—such as anatomy, composition, and blade location—to select the right knife. The following section explains these characteristics so you can proceed with confidence.

CARBON STEEL BLADE

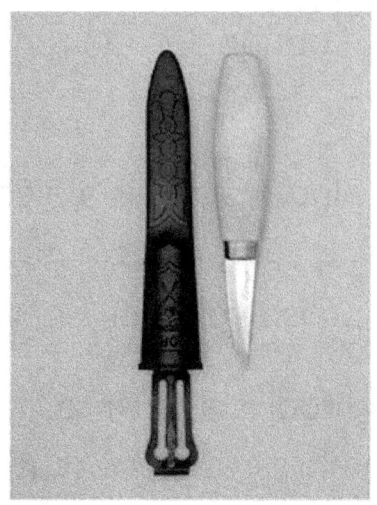

Most good whittling knives are made of carbon steel. This is a softer steel than stainless, so it's easier to sharpen and holds a sharper edge. The downsides are that you will need to sharpen it often, and the blade can rust and tarnish if it gets wet. Honing your carbon steel blade regularly and keeping it dry will ensure it lasts a lifetime. If you are unsure what steel your knife is made of, look near the maker's stamp on the blade for the word "carbon" or "stainless".

BLADE LOCATION

There are two main types of whittling knives: fixed blade knives and folding knives. Folding knives, such as pocketknives, offer affordability and portability. However, the handles are not very ergonomic, making them difficult to use for extended periods of time. They often have a different bevel type running the blade width, with a micro bevel on the edge to make them sharp. This makes them more difficult to whittle with properly, and often makes them less sharp. A fixed-blade knife offers more comfort and ease of use but tends to be more expensive. Regardless of which type of knife you get, look for one with a blade length ranging from two to four inches.

LOCKING BLADES

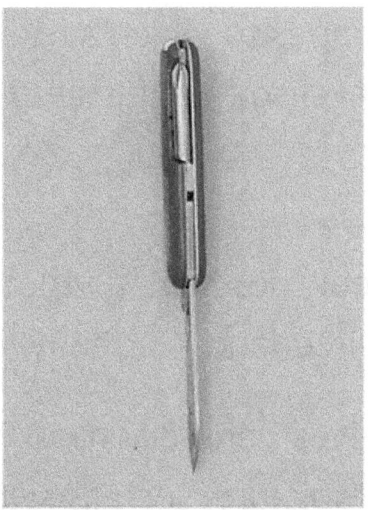

If you decide to use a folding knife, purchase one with a locking blade. Many cheaper folding knives rely on friction and positioning to keep the blade open. These knives can be extremely dangerous to use for whittling because the blade can pop out of position and close on your fingers. Look for a folding knife with a locking blade and a separate mechanism to unlock the blade.

WHAT TO CONSIDER WHEN CHOOSING YOUR KNIFE

When selecting knives, first decide how much you want to spend. Several have luxury characteristics that are nice if you are invested in whittling but are not necessary for a beginner carver. The following list explains key features to consider for each level of knife quality.

BASIC:

REPUTABLE BRAND: Choose a knife from a reputable brand, not a knockoff, to ensure that the blade does not break while using it.

ERGONOMIC HANDLE: You'll want to select a handle that fits well in your hand so that whittling is comfortable.

BEVEL: There are several shapes to which a bevel can be ground. You'll want a straight-ground bevel so that it is easy to sharpen.

MID-RANGE:

COUNTRY OF ORIGIN: Some countries have a reputation for high-quality steel, such as Sweden, Switzerland, Germany, and Japan.

WOODEN HANDLE: Quality knives generally have wooden handles. Unlike plastic, wood will absorb moisture, such as sweat from your palms, making for a more enjoyable whittling experience.

STEEL TYPE: Historically, carbon steel has been used for whittling because it can achieve a sharper edge and is easy to sharpen. However, it is also important to consider your circumstances. Stainless steel is harder, meaning you need to sharpen it relatively less often, and it will not rust.

HIGH-END:

HANDMADE: Some of the nicest blades on the market are hand-forged by independent blacksmiths. Be sure to look for a knife made by a toolmaker who is also a whittler.

HOLLOW-GROUND BEVEL: This bevel type is concave in cross-section, making it sharper. It requires a slightly different, albeit fast, sharpening technique.

HANDLE WOOD TYPE: Luxury knives have hardwood handles such as cherry, walnut, or curly maple.

TANG: The tang is the part of the blade within the handle. Luxury knives have a full tang, meaning the blade continues through the whole handle, offering strength and balance.

Reliable Brands

A good knife is the most crucial tool in your whittling kit, and selecting a quality whittling knife has become challenging. It's important to know the reliable brands because many low-quality knockoffs are available. Plenty of independent toolmakers worldwide offer high-quality, handmade knives. Those are often more expensive, so if you are just getting started, the following brands are a great budget-friendly place to begin.

SWISS ARMY KNIVES: When we think of whittling, we think of Swiss Army knives. These handy folding knives are portable and are exceptionally durable. If you do most of your whittling while on camping trips, they are a great option.

MORAKNIV OF SWEDEN: Known to most whittlers as Mora knives, these blades are perfect for everything from whittling to bushcraft. They are made from high-quality carbon or stainless steel (be sure to double-check before you purchase). Most of the knives cost under $30 and will last you a lifetime. They have flat bevels that are easy to sharpen, and most come with ergonomic wooden handles for hours of enjoyable whittling.

FLEXCUT KNIVES: Flexcut makes knives and detail gouges that are great for beginners. They also make sharpening systems specific to their knives, which are an invaluable addition to your whittling kit. Flexcut knives are made in the United States and come in a wide range of options, including folding knives, detail knives, gouges, and straight knives.

BÜTZ: These knives, designed and used by Rick Bütz, have specialized handles that are easy to hold, providing a safe and efficient whittling experience. They offer two blade shapes, one for roughing out and one for details; both are designed with the whittler in mind. Unfortunately, they are no longer in production, but you can often find used ones online.

Sharpening Your Knives

A sharp knife can be the difference between safe, enjoyable whittling and a frustrating, more dangerous experience. The following steps will help you keep your knife sharp for all of the projects in this book. You won't need to do all three steps every time you sharpen. Whichever step you start with, you will need to do all the steps after it in order to have a sharp knife.

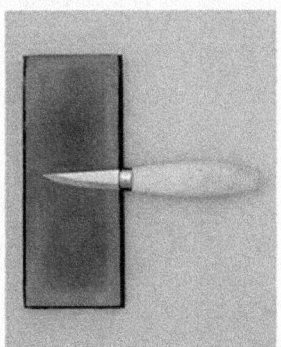

1. **Correct the edge geometry:** This is necessary when your blade has major nicks or rounded edges. The angled section of the blade that makes it sharp is called the bevel. Each bevel has a set, consistent angle, which you maintain by removing enough steel behind the deepest imperfection to create the new edge. Set the bevel flat on the rough side of the stone and pull the blade across the stone with consistent angle, pressure, and passes. Repeat on both sides until all imperfections are removed.

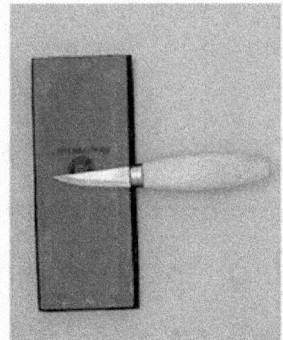

2. **Hone the edge:** Honing will correct minor but visible imperfections that do not require the rough side of the stone. Perform step 1, but with the smooth side of the whetstone. A

small amount of steel, called a burr, will be pushed up and over your blade, indicating that you have made enough passes on one side. Repeat on each side, making fewer passes each time, until the burr has been removed completely.

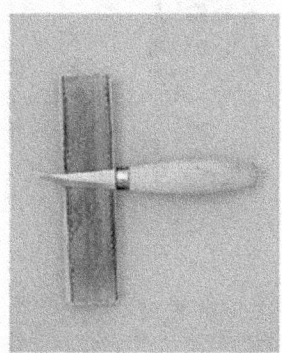

3. **Polish the edge:** Do this when your blade has no visible imperfections, but it is not cutting as well as it used to. The technique is the same as in the previous steps, but uses a strop instead of a whetstone. Keep making passes until the blade feels smooth on both sides. This step should be done frequently and can prevent steps 1 and 2 from being necessary for many weeks, or months, of regular whittling.

Knife and Whittling Safety

Using a sharp blade will always carry some risk, regardless of how skilled you become at whittling. The following safety tips will help you reduce that risk for a safer, more worry-free whittling experience.

FIRST AID KIT: Having a first aid kit, and the knowledge of how to use it, is the best way to ensure a safe carving experience. Your kit should include bandages, antiseptic wipes, triple antibiotic ointment (such as

Neosporin), gauze pads, and medical tape. If you are not feeling confident in your first aid skills, take a first aid course; most local municipalities offer one.

TAKE CARE WHEN SHEATHING AND UNSHEATHING YOUR KNIFE: One of the most dangerous times in your whittling is when you sheathe and unsheathe your knife because you are either excited to begin or tired from hours of whittling fun. Always sheathe and unsheathe your knife slowly and carefully to avoid injury.

CARVE DOWN AND AWAY FROM YOURSELF: Although some more advanced knife techniques, like the paring cut, appear to require carving toward yourself, they are just more subtle forms of carving away from yourself. Always consider the path of your knife, and make sure there are no knees, fingers, hands, other people, or pets in the way.

KEEP A FIRM GRIP: Always keep a fist grip on your knife handle and your project. This keeps your thumbs out of the way and avoids slipping accidents. Some techniques (like the paring cut and the push cut) will require you to intentionally unlock your thumb to use it as an anchor.

STAY SHARP: Always keep a sharp mind and a sharp blade when you whittle. Never whittle when you are tired, angry, or frustrated. A dull knife is dangerous because it requires more force to make your cuts, giving you less control. This can make accidents more severe. Therefore, it is important to sharpen your knives regularly and correctly.

Selecting Wood

Wood is the most common material used in whittling and is the sole material used in this book. Unlike other materials, like soap and wax, wood is arranged in a series of fibers, known as grain. You will swiftly notice the difference between whittling "with the grain" versus "against the grain." Your knife is a tiny wedge, like a splitting tool. When you carve against the grain, you push the wedge between these fibers, causing mini splits and rips. When you carve with the grain, the blade floats across the fibers, shaving them off evenly.

TYPES OF WOOD FOR WHITTLING

There are several factors to consider when selecting carving wood: strength, hardness, porosity (meaning how smooth or rough it will look when finished), and appearance. Basswood is ideal for whittling because it's soft, yet strong, and finishes nicely. It's also relatively inexpensive and can be found in most craft and hardware stores. Birch is similar to basswood but can be harder and is less widely available. Conifers are often called softwoods and are a good choice for beginners because they are easy to carve. However, they can sometimes be too weak for thin projects, and some species are very resinous.

As you progress in your whittling hobby, you may want to explore other hardwoods. Maple is light in color and often has iridescent flecks. It is not very porous, so it finishes beautifully, although it is much harder than basswood and birch. Oak is a very hard wood that is often quite porous (especially red oak). It has a beautiful color and "rays" that radiate from the center of the log to the outside, giving it a striped appearance. Cherry and walnut are great options if you want beautiful wood grain and don't mind carving dense wood. Walnut is more porous than cherry and contains silicates that can dull your tools.

WHERE TO GET YOUR MATERIALS

You can find wood for whittling in many different stores. The store that's best for you depends on your location and budget and the tools you have on hand. Hardware stores are a reliable source for dowels and short sections of lumber. They are generally geared to a do-it-yourself/home improvement audience, so the selection might not be ideal for whittling. Art and craft stores usually have a whittling section with basswood in exact dimensions, so you do not need any power tools to get started. Shopping at these stores is a bit more expensive than shopping at a lumberyard but cheaper than buying a table saw. Local lumber mills are one of the cheapest options and are ideal for someone with power tools to resize lumber to the correct dimensions. The salespeople are often knowledgeable and can answer your questions to steer you in the right direction. In some places, they will cut the pieces down for you if you ask nicely.

WOOD IN THE WILD

The wild, with more than 640 tree species in the United States alone, offers a vast selection of wood for whittling. You can improve the health of the forest by removing downed and dying trees. Many vertical trees are important habitats for wildlife and can be dangerous to fell, so it is best to harvest wood that has already fallen. Harvesting or gathering from most public lands is illegal, so always check the laws where you want to harvest, or stick to your own private land. Transporting wood across county lines is often prohibited in order to reduce the spread of invasive species.

PROJECT STARTER DIMENSIONS

The projects in this book can be done with either dimensional wood or irregular wood from the wild. Each project will detail the starting length, width, and depth. If you purchase materials from a craft store or a lumberyard, you should buy wood with a width and depth similar to those specified for the project. If needed, you can make pieces shorter with your hand saw. When sawing, be sure to measure the correct length and draw a guideline around the whole piece to ensure accurate, square sawing.

If you are harvesting your own wood, you will likely need some extra hand tools to process a tree into a whittling block with the correct dimensions. In addition to a folding saw, you will want a controlled splitting tool, such as splitting wedges or a hatchet and a wooden mallet. First, saw the log to the correct length, and then split it to the correct width and depth.

Some projects start with cylindrical wood dimensions, meaning you can begin with either a wooden dowel or a stick that is free of knots, relatively fresh, and rot-free. Here, diameter and length are the most important measurements.

Basic Whittling Shapes and Cuts

Now that you have the perfect whittling knife and wood pieces and know all the rules of knife safety, it's time to practice the fundamental whittling techniques. The following techniques are the basic cuts that will be combined to make all of the projects in this book. In the following chapters, each project step will name the technique to use without re-explaining it, so you should refer back to this section any time you need a refresher or until you build your confidence.

SAMPLER

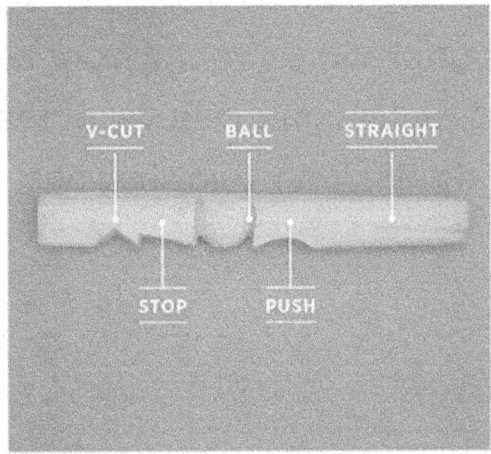

A sampler is a stick or a piece of wood on which a whittler can practice a technique before jumping into a project. It can also be a quick reference if you use it to make and label each of the cuts described below and keep it in your whittling kit. Make as many samplers as you want in order to gain confidence with each technique. For the best results, use a straight-grained, rectangular piece of basswood about 8 inches long and 1 inch wide.

STRAIGHT CUT

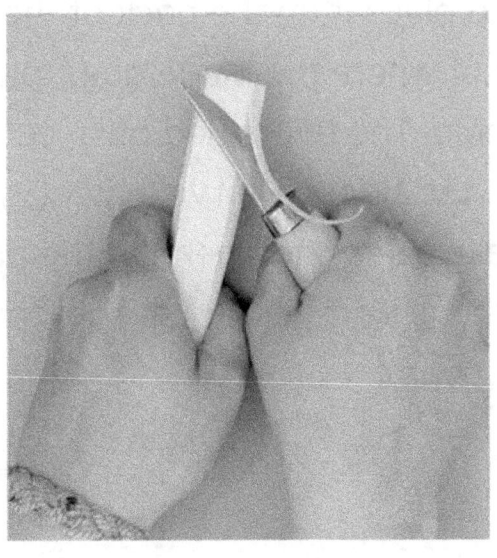

The straight cut is the most basic and common whittling technique. It is great for carving long, straight areas of projects. Hold the back half of your project with a fist grip, and carve the front half, keeping a fist grip on your knife handle as well. Align the bevel of the blade so it just catches the wood and whittle long, thin shavings.

PUSH CUT

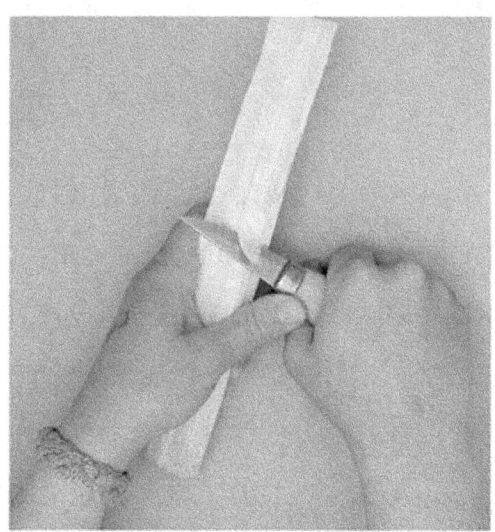

A push cut is a powerful yet controlled way to round the ends of your project. Starting with a fist grip with both hands, unlock the thumb holding the project and place it on the back of the blade handle. With your thumb in control of where the blade goes, push the knife forward, carving a short woodchip. The two-sided push cut will make a U-shaped cut when viewed from the side. To carve a divot, start in the middle of the piece of wood, make a shaving, then flip the project and meet your woodchip from the other side, releasing it from the wood. Repeat until you reach the desired depth.

V-CUT (OR V-SHAPED CUT)

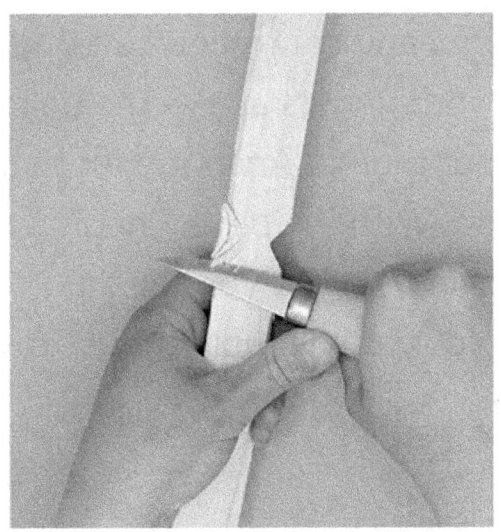

A v-cut (or v-shaped cut) will carve a two-sided angle into the wood that is v-shaped when looked at from the side. Begin by drawing three parallel, equidistant lines around the stick. Starting at line one, carve down into the wood at an angle toward the middle line (line two). Flip the stick around and repeat from line three to line two. This will release the woodchip from the first cut, leaving behind a triangular depression in the wood.

PARING CUT

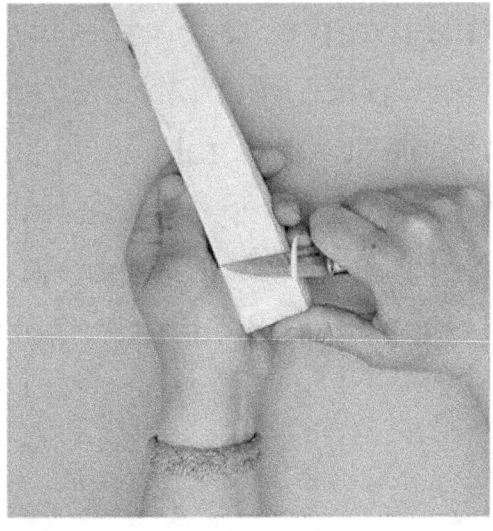

A paring cut is a powerful and controlled cut. Begin by holding the handle of the blade in your fingers above the palm knuckles, with the blade facing toward your thumb. Anchor your thumb on the end of your project, below the wood. With the bevel lined up on the wood, close your fist to carve a shaving toward your anchored thumb. The blade's path should go above your thumb, not straight toward it, but you may want to use a safety glove.

STOP CUT

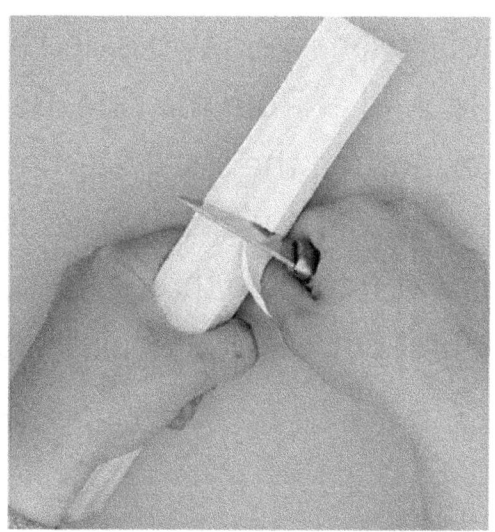

A stop cut, created with a two-part technique, is shaped like a 7 when viewed from the side. First, place your blade at a 90-degree angle to the piece of wood, perpendicular to the grain lines, and make a shallow cut into the wood with moderate pressure. Be careful to maintain control and not rock or slide the blade. Then, in a second cut, carve toward the angled cut, releasing a chip of wood. Repeat until you have achieved the desired depth.

BALL CUT

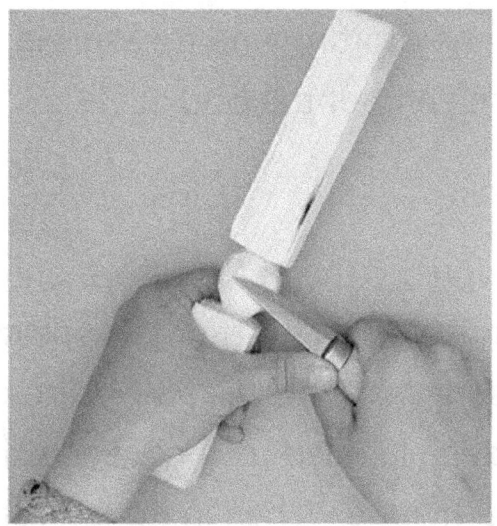

A ball cut is great for spoon bowls and eggs and for adding decorative elements to handles. Begin with a cylindrical piece of wood that has a section in the middle as wide as it is long (for instance, a 1-inch section in the middle of a 1-inch-diameter dowel). Use the push cut to whittle shavings from the midpoint to the end, rotating the wood with each cut. Then, inch forward and repeat at a steeper angle until one side of the cylinder is spherical. Then, flip the wood around and repeat on the other side. Because you will be carving in the middle of a length of wood, you will want to release the woodchips with a stop cut.

Patterns and Their Purpose

Patterns are premade whittling guides that help you achieve more complicated projects without needing advanced drawing or design skills. They are a terrific way to provide proportion, shape, and guidelines for details, allowing you to whittle complex and impressive designs. Patterns will also help you carve multiples of the same design consistently. Some of the more advanced projects contained here have patterns to save you time drafting and measuring. All patterns in this book are available at the end of the book.

PATTERN KEY

All the shapes and designs of the patterns are only suggestions, and you are welcome to customize and alter them as you see fit. The directional arrows for carving ensure that you will always be carving with the grain. The pattern here has been labeled to show each shape and its corresponding knife technique. When in doubt, refer to this key as a quick guide, or you can also read the written instructions of your project.

	KEY
↓	**Carving direction**
‖	**Grain orientation**
– – –	**Switch carving direction**
↓	**Straight cut**
⇗	**Push cut**
⇘	**V-shape cut**
⟲	**Ball cut**
⌐┐	**Stop cut**

APPLYING A PATTERN

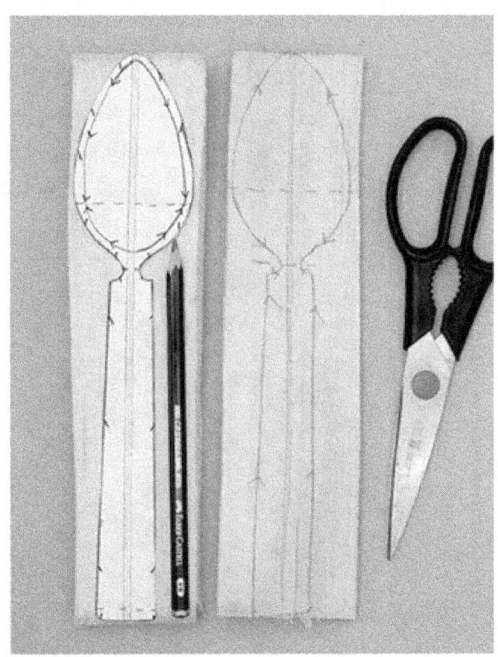

The patterns in this book can be traced. Each pattern is designed to fit on a block of wood with the dimensions detailed at the beginning of its project. Once printed, cut out the pattern and trace it onto the front of the wood block you want to carve. Feel free to cut out the details on each pattern or draw them freehand. Line up the pattern with the wood grain running vertically for the directional arrows for carving to be correct. Then, transfer the directional arrows to your wood block. Once the pattern has been transferred, keep it near you for quick reference. You may want to redraw some lines that get whittled off.

Finishing Touches

An easy way to add some personal touches to your piece, or give it a more polished look, is to apply some finishing techniques. These techniques are not required for any of the projects in this book and should be thought of as bonus steps. Some finishing techniques increase the durability and longevity of your finished project, and others are just for looks. Some of the nicest projects I have seen are unfinished, so don't feel you need to apply these techniques to make a great piece.

OILING will make your project shine and increase its durability and longevity. Oil fills in the wood pores and highlights the grain. Some oils will polymerize (known colloquially as "drying"), meaning they react with oxygen to form a solid, waterproof surface that is great for utensils or any carving that will go outside. If you are using oil for utensils, apply one that is food safe, like tung oil, and allow it to dry completely before using. Avoid olive oil for anything that will get wet because it can go rancid quickly.

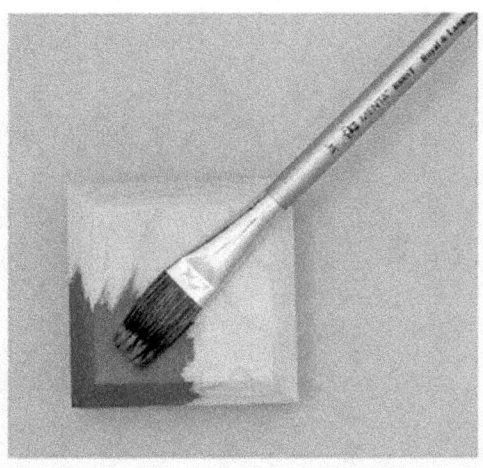

PAINTING is a simple way to add some color and define certain project features. Acrylic paint is inexpensive and comes in a wide array of colors. It forms a nice, even coat and can be thinned with water for a more transparent stain. Milk paint is a great option for utensils because it's a nontoxic, porous paint that moves with the wood and is unlikely to chip with use and washing.

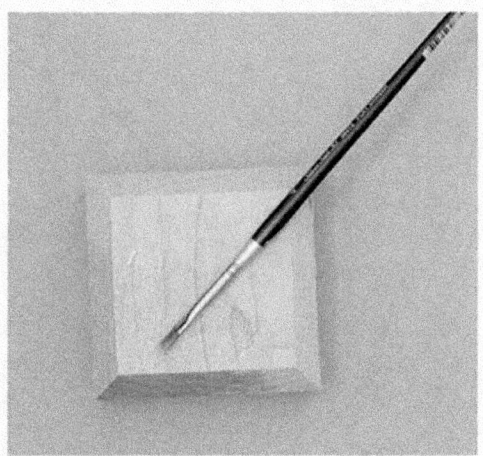

POLYURETHANE is a liquid, plastic coating that cures into a waterproof finish and is great if your piece will live outside. Brush it on with multiple thin coats and follow the specific drying times on the product label.

SANDING is likely the finishing technique you will use most often. Start with a low-grit (100 to 120) sandpaper square, and sand your entire project to the desired shape. Then, use a medium-grit (220) smoothing paper to remove the previous sand marks. Finish with a higher grit (400 to 600) to give your piece a smooth finish. It's helpful to either oil or stain your project after sanding.

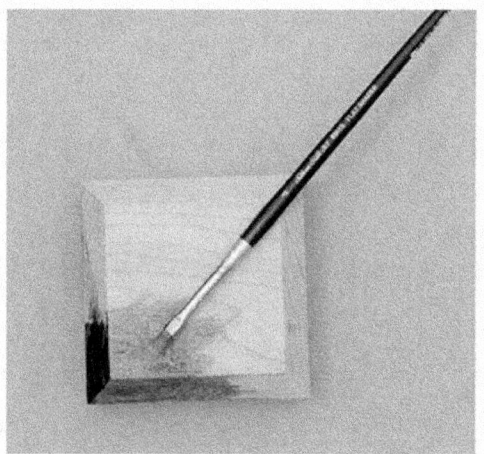

STAINING a project will deepen the color and shine of the wood and make it more resistant to the elements. This is a great option if you chose a soft wood without an interesting grain color. Always follow the specific directions on the product label for best results.

About the Projects

Now that you know all the basics, you are ready to get whittling! The following projects have been carefully selected to guide you on your whittling journey. They become more complex as your skills increase.

- Chapter 2 contains simple, practical projects that will help you hone a few core skills at a time. Each of these projects can be completed in under an hour, with only a handful of steps, and require just a few simple tools and materials.

- Chapter 3 explores more three-dimensional projects, like figure carving, that you can jump into once you have practiced the basic techniques in chapter 2. This chapter details a mix of shorter and longer projects.

- Chapter 4 projects are more complex, but they are described with more steps and a template to make them beginner-friendly. These projects will encourage you to combine all the skills you build in chapters 2 and 3.

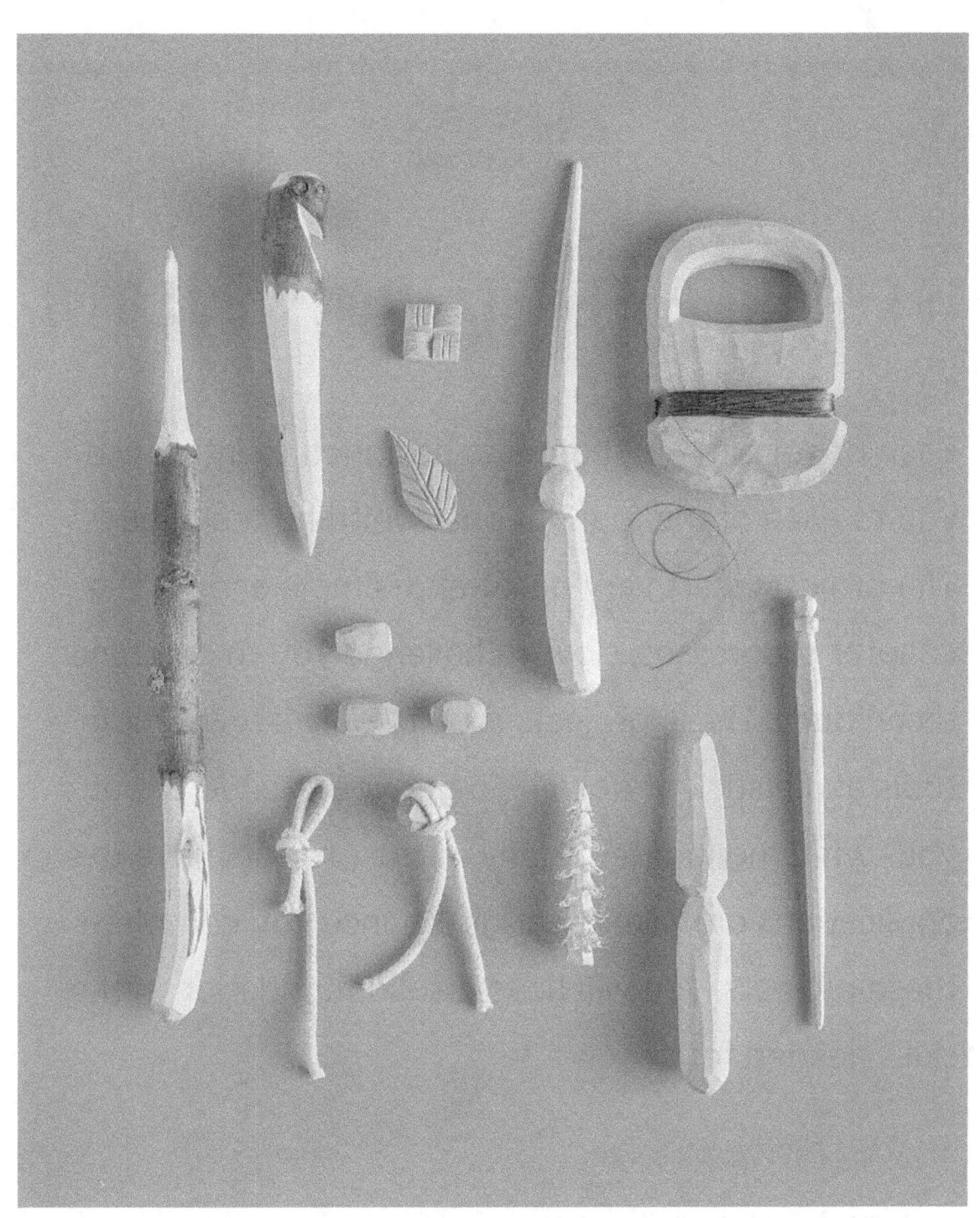

TWO

BEGINNER WHITTLING PROJECTS

Each project in this chapter is designed to introduce you to each of the foundational whittling techniques. The projects start very quick-and-simple and, as the chapter progresses, slowly challenge you to combine techniques. These projects require only a few simple tools and a stick or dowel. To get you excited about your whittling journey, many of the projects have useful applications or make great gifts. Once you complete these projects, you will have a solid foundation in the skills needed for chapter 3.

- Simple Butter Spreader
- S'mores Roasting Stick
- Whittled Toggles
- Whittled Tent Stake
- Magic Wand

- **Hairpin**
- **Leaf Pendant**
- **Whittled Trees**
- **Simple Fishing Handline**

Simple Butter Spreader

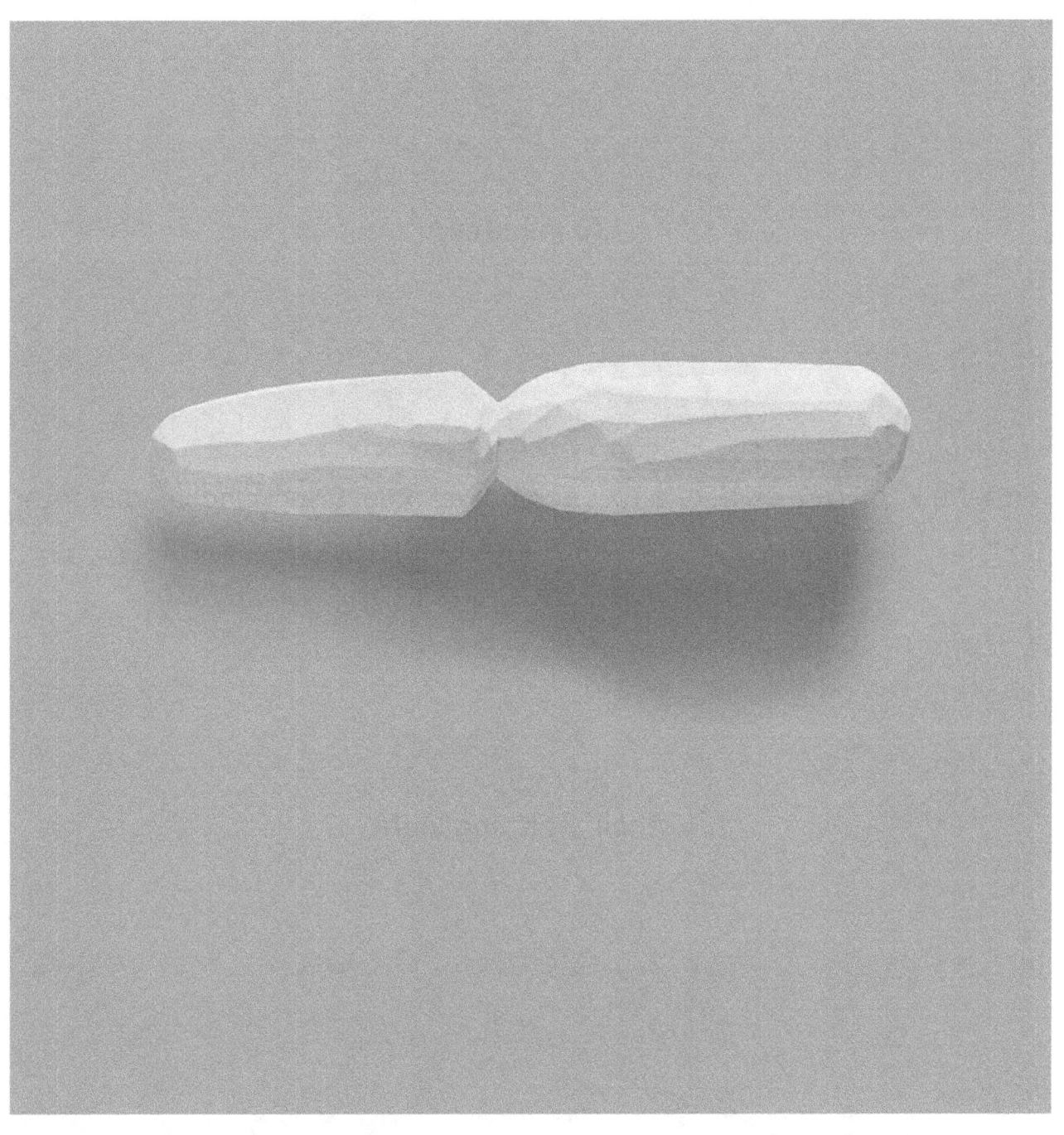

This camping essential can be carved from nearly any stick. This beginner project offers practice with the straight cut, v-cut, and push cut.

START-TO-FINISH TIME:
30 minutes

WOOD DIMENSIONS:
Either a knot-free stick or a wooden dowel measuring 1 inch in diameter and 7 inches long

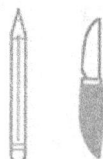

SUPPLIES:
Pencil, whittling knife

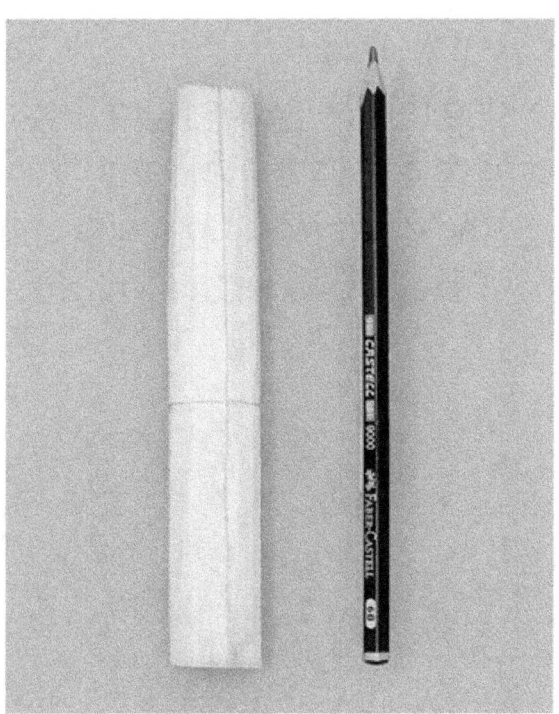

1. Draw guidelines. Begin by drawing two 7-inch lines lengthwise on opposite sides of the stick. Then, draw a perpendicular line around the stick at the midway point. These lines will help you whittle a straight spreader with an even transition from handle to blade.

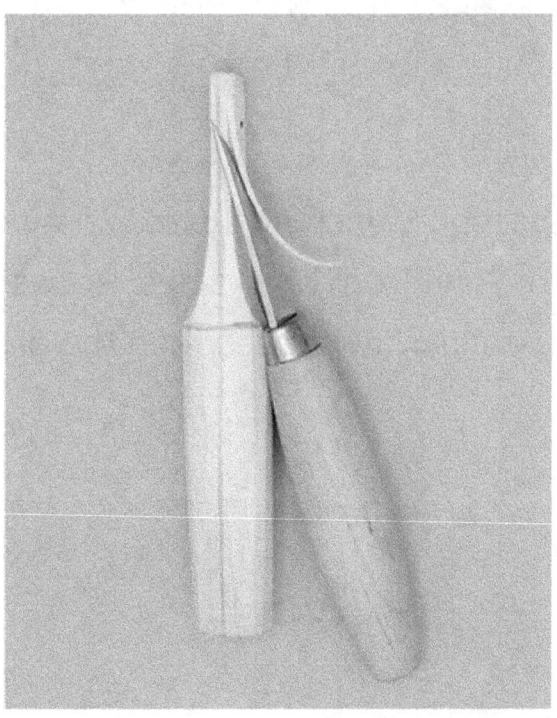

2. Flatten both sides of the spreader's "blade." Start by using the straight cut to whittle long thin shavings from the midpoint to the end of the stick. Once you have a flat surface, rotate the spreader 180 degrees, and repeat on the other side. Continue until the spreader's thickness (about ⅓ inch) is even, using the lengthwise guidelines for reference.

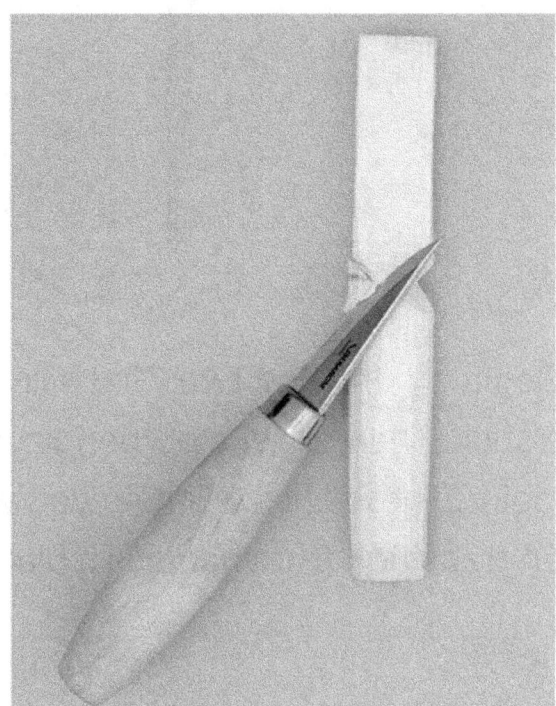

3. Shape the intersection between the blade and the handle. On the unwhittled portion, starting ¼ inch away from the midpoint, use the v-cut to carve toward the line from both sides. Repeat all the way around the stick until there is a clear divide between the blade and the handle.

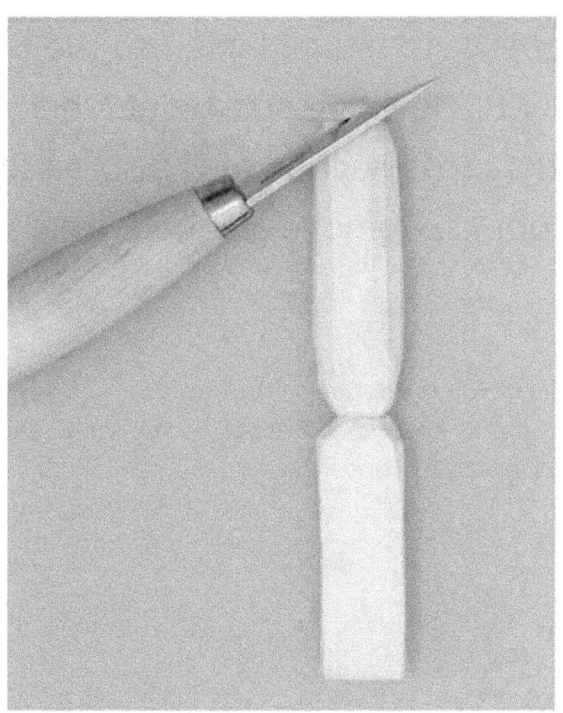

4. Round the handle. Holding the blade end of your spreader, use the push cut to round the back of your spreader's handle. Work all the way around the stick with small cuts to remove the hard corners. You can remove the bark on the handle or leave it for a rustic look.

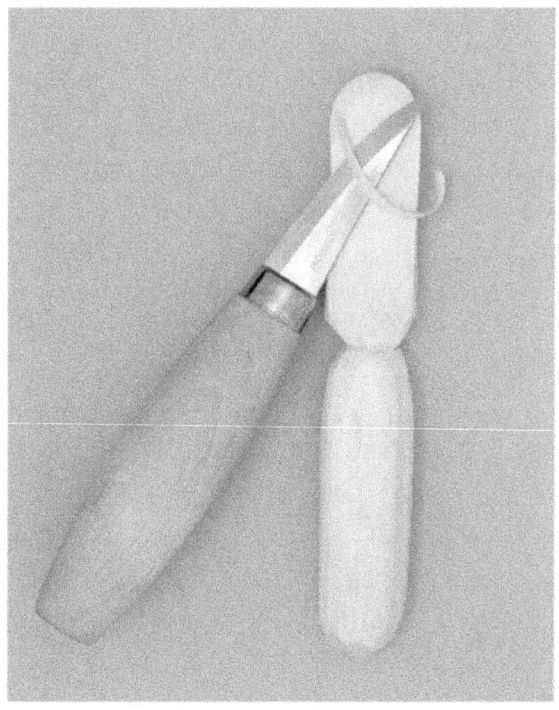

5. Shape the blade point and bevel. First, use the push cut to whittle the tip of the spreader blade into a soft point. Then, use a push cut to angle either side so the cross-section of the spreader blade is a diamond shape with rounded points. Remove any bark from the edges of the spreader's blade.

> **TECHNIQUE TIP:** You can draw a guideline without a straight edge by holding the pencil at the center point, anchoring your hand on the edge of the stick, and sliding your hand and the pencil together down the stick's length.

S'mores Roasting Stick

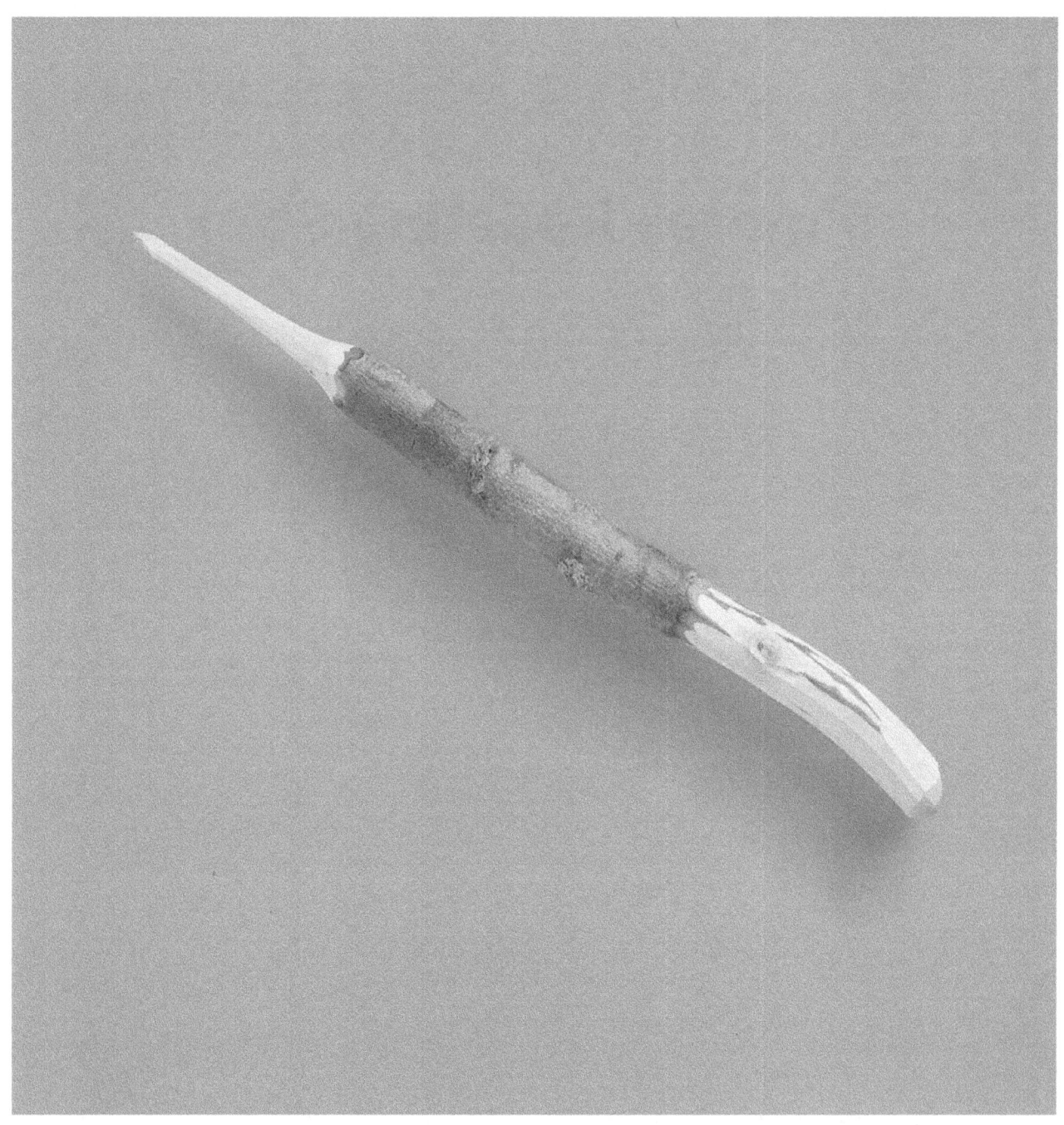

The campfire experience is not complete without s'mores. This simple project will enhance your marshmallow-roasting abilities while offering practice with the straight cut and push cut.

START-TO-FINISH TIME:
15 minutes

WOOD DIMENSIONS:
Either a knot-free stick or a wooden dowel measuring at least 14 inches long and approximately 1 inch in diameter. Using green wood will help prevent the stick from burning.

SUPPLIES:
Whittling knife

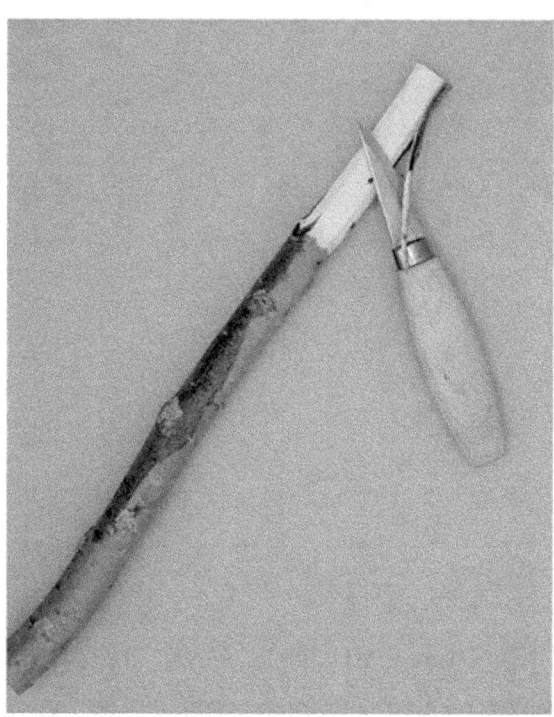

1. Remove the bark from the front 4 inches. Use the straight cut to carefully remove the bark from the roasting end of the stick. Be sure to hold the back half of your project and whittle the front half down and away from yourself.

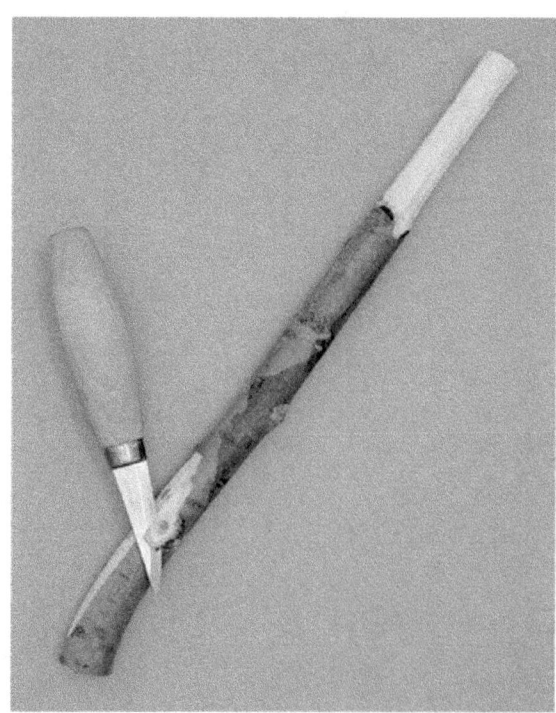

2. Whittle the handle. Whittle the bottom 4 inches from the opposite end of the roasting stick into a comfortable handle by removing any bumps or knots. Begin with the straight cut to remove the bark, and then use the push cut to remove knots.

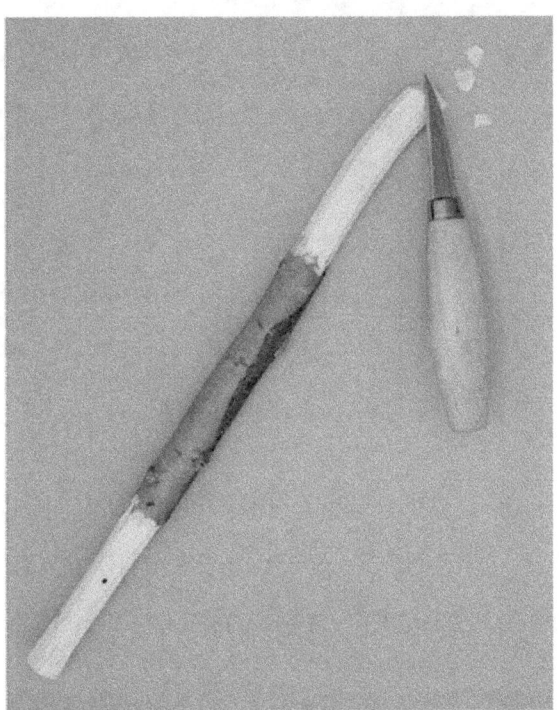

3. Round the back of the handle. Use the push cut to round the back of the handle. Rotate the stick slightly with each pass to achieve a consistent, rounded handle.

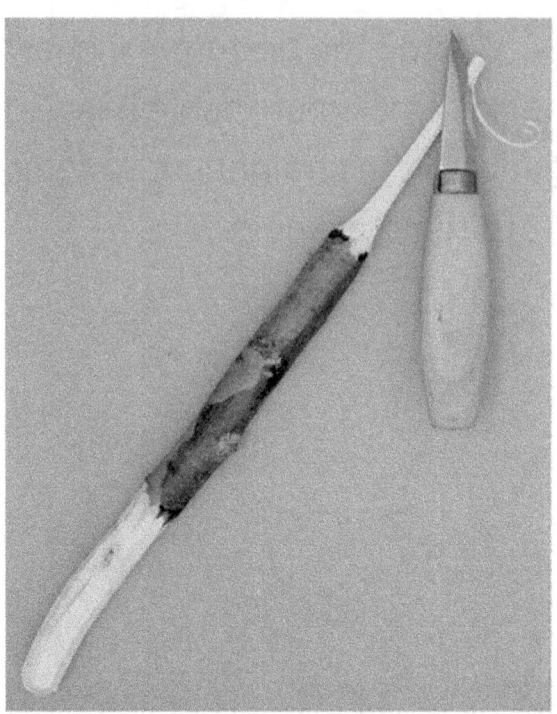

4. Thin the roasting end. The front 4 inches will hold the marshmallows, so making that section thin and even is essential. Use the straight cut to thin this section to about ¼ inch in diameter.

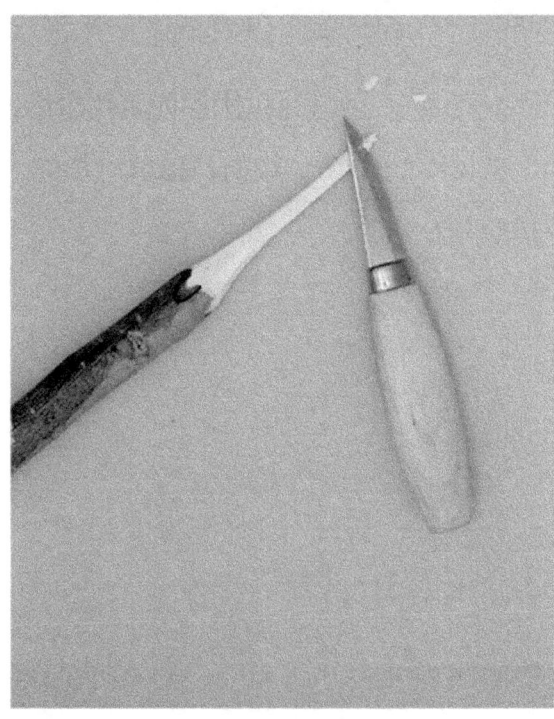

5. Whittle a point on the roasting end. Use the push cut to whittle the roasting end of the stick into a consistent point. Rotate the stick with each cut to keep the point centered.

> **MIX IT UP TIP:** Try looking for a branched y-shaped stick and whittle multiple working ends to roast many marshmallows at once. No oil or finish should be used on roasting sticks, which are being placed near fire.

Whittled Toggles

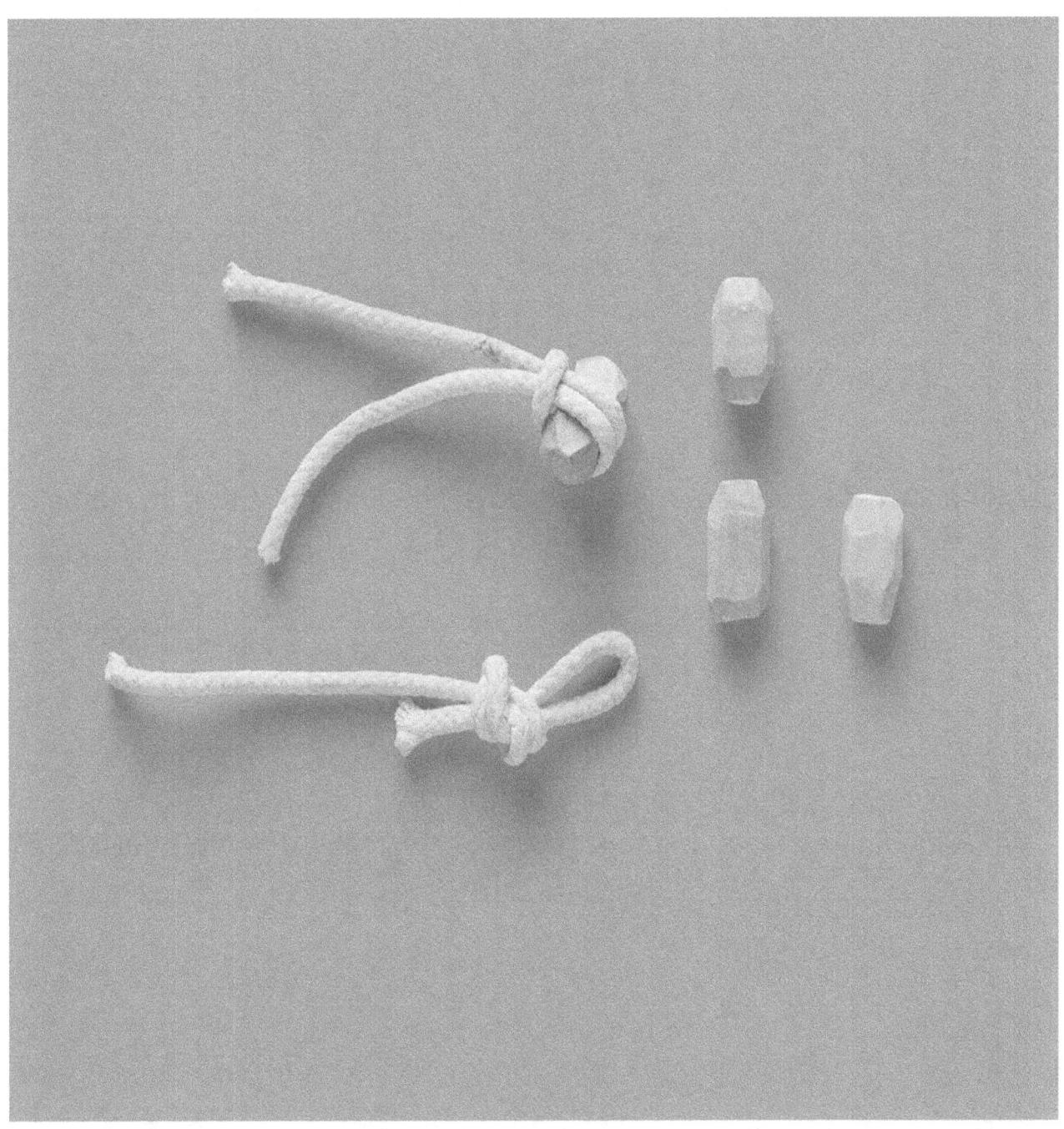

Toggles are simple pegs and rope loops that work like a clasp on a necklace and are a clever way to hold gear on your pack.

START-TO-FINISH TIME:
15 minutes per toggle

WOOD DIMENSIONS:
Either a knot-free stick or a wooden dowel measuring ½ inch in diameter and 6 inches long

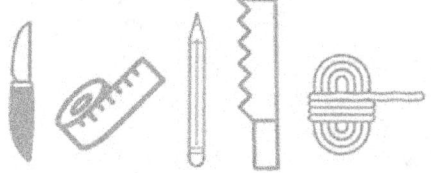

SUPPLIES:
Whittling knife, measuring tape, pencil, saw, small-diameter cord (like paracord)

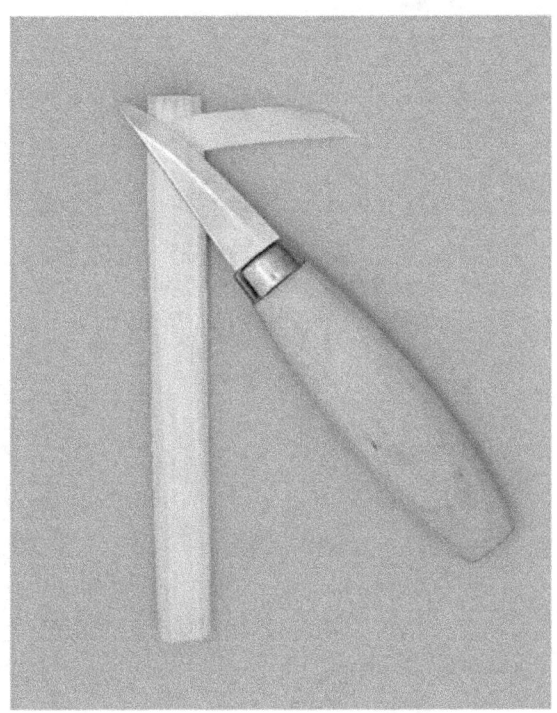

1. Flatten two parallel sides of the stick. Hold the back half of the stick or dowel and work the front half. Use a straight cut to flatten one side of the stick. Flip the project around and flatten the other half. When the entire stick has a flat side, rotate it 180 degrees and repeat on the other side.

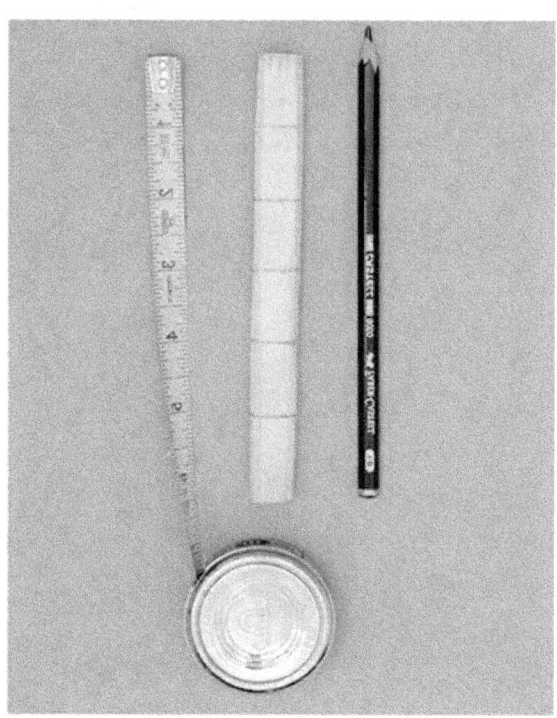

2. Measure and mark the toggles. With your measuring tape and pencil, mark horizontal guidelines every 1 inch down your stick or dowel. Each section will be its own toggle, with an inch of waste wood on each end so you can safely hold the project. A 6-inch stick will make four toggles.

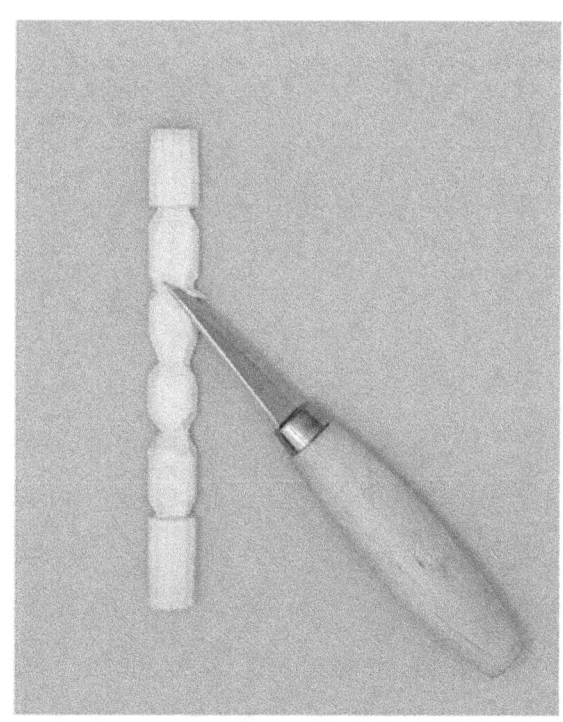

3. Distinguish between each toggle with a v-cut. Use your guidelines as the meeting point for the v-cut to distinguish between each toggle. When they are separated, the toggles will have rounded ends. The outer two lines can be distinguished with a stop cut because the waste wood will be sawn off.

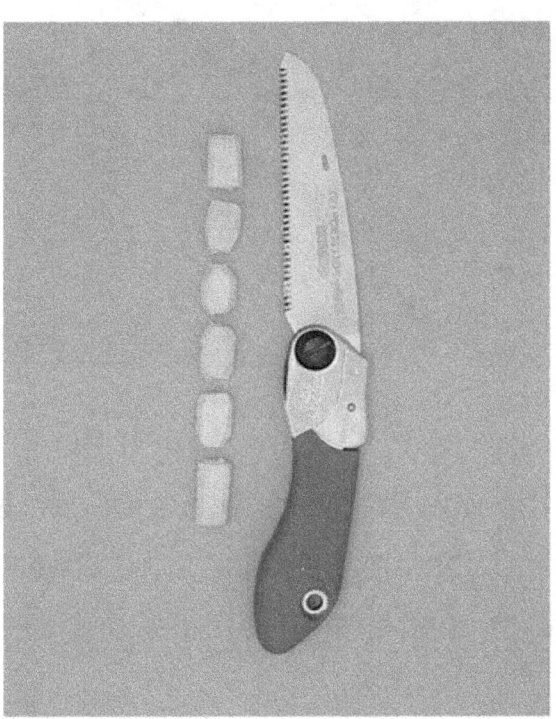

4. Separate each toggle. Secure your project and carefully saw apart each toggle. Take care to move your saw forward and back, angling straight down. Pressing the saw into the wood will cause the saw to get stuck.

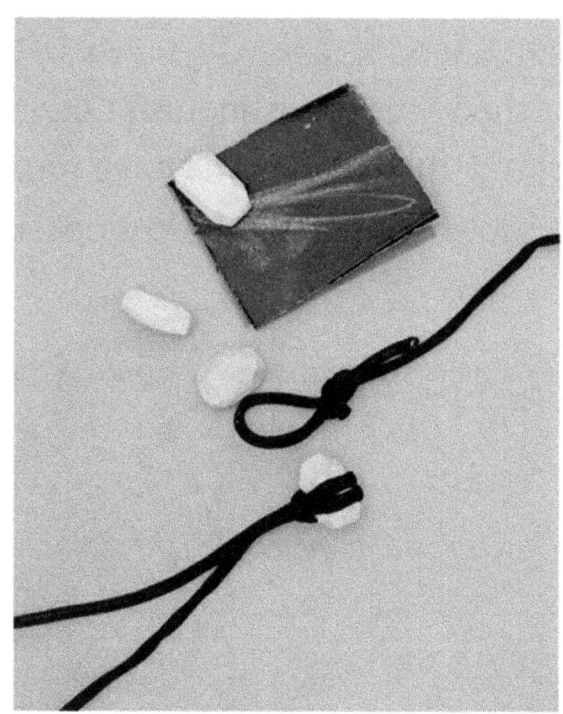

5. Shape the ends and tie on the paracord. If the ends of the toggles look rough, smooth them with low-grit sandpaper. Make a slip knot at the end of the cord and secure it around the center of each toggle. Tie a loop in another piece of cord that just fits over the toggle.

> **PERSONALIZE IT TIP:** To ensure that the paracord is secured, you can carve a divot in the center of each toggle. Do this using the two-sided push cut before separating the toggles in step 4.

Whittled Tent Stake

A tent stake is a useful project that does not require precise lines or measurements and is best whittled while sitting around a campfire.

START-TO-FINISH TIME:
30 minutes

WOOD DIMENSIONS:
Either a knot-free stick or a wooden dowel measuring 1 inch in diameter and 6 to 8 inches long

SUPPLIES:
Whittling knife

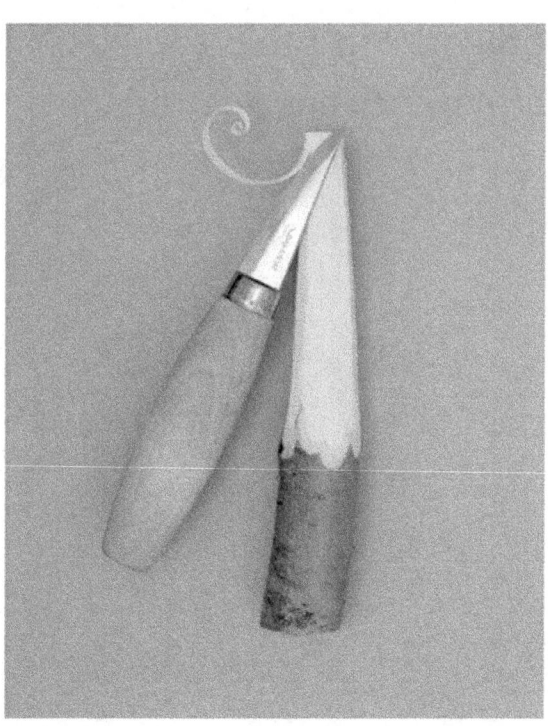

1. Taper the stake. Use the straight cut to taper the bottom two-thirds of the stake so it will go into the ground more easily. Carve long, thin shavings while paying attention to consistency and rotating the stick slightly with each pass.

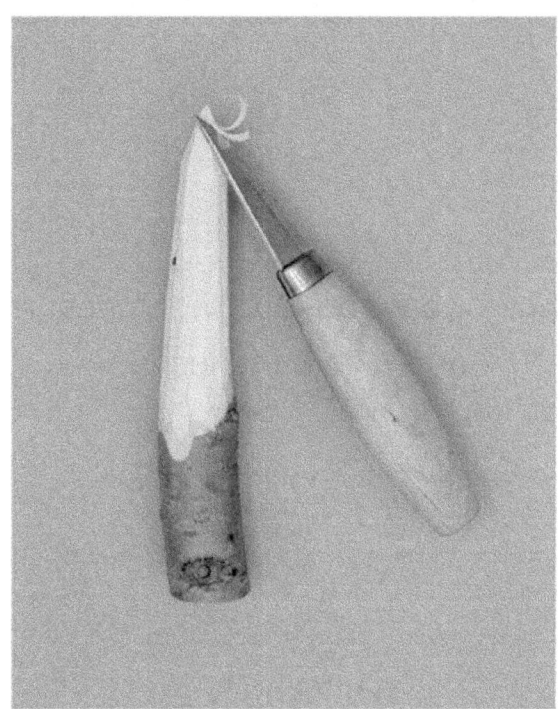

2. Point the end. Use the push cut to point the final inch of the tapered end. Rotate the stake with each cut, keeping the point centered on the stick.

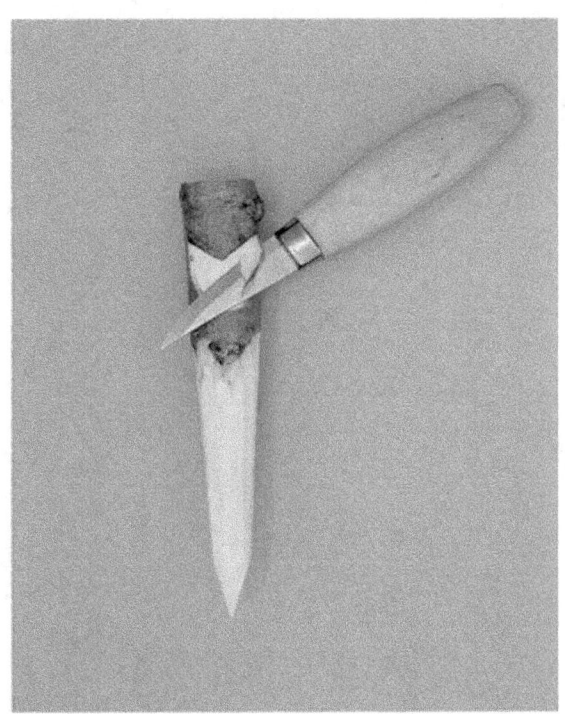

3. Carve the notch for the tent lines. Using two angled stop cuts, whittle a downward-pointing, triangular notch located near the top third of the stake. This notch will hold the tent line to the stake. Position your stop cuts so that each of the 90-degree cuts is on top, and then carve toward them from the base.

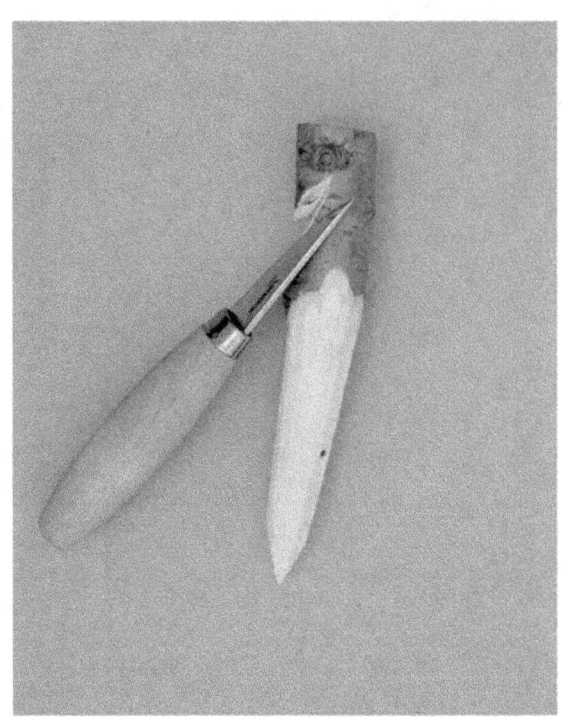

4. Undercut the notch. Undercutting is the process of carving an overhang on any cut. It will help hold the tent line more securely. Continue with the stop cut technique on the notch and begin to adjust the 90-degree angle deeper until there is a pronounced overhang.

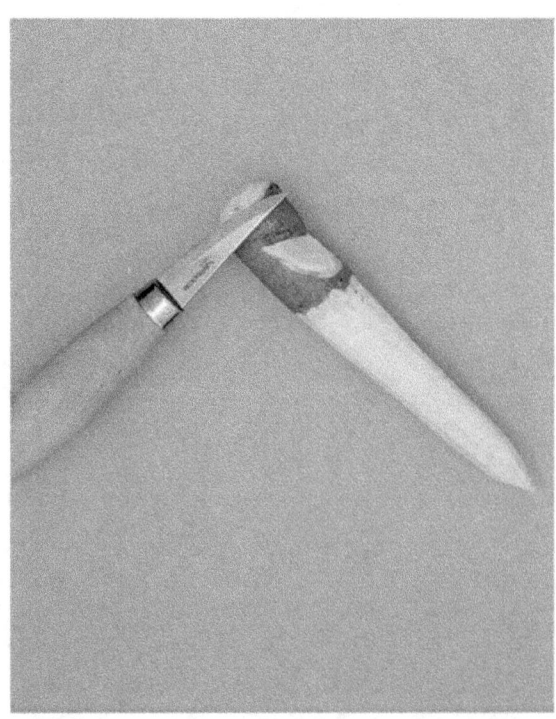

5. Round the top. Round the top with the push cut to make your tent stake safer and more aesthetically pleasing. Rotate the stick with each cut to achieve a consistent, rounded top.

> **TIP:** Bark can give your piece a rustic look, or it can hinder its functionality. If the bark is slipping easily off the stick, it's best to remove it.

Magic Wand

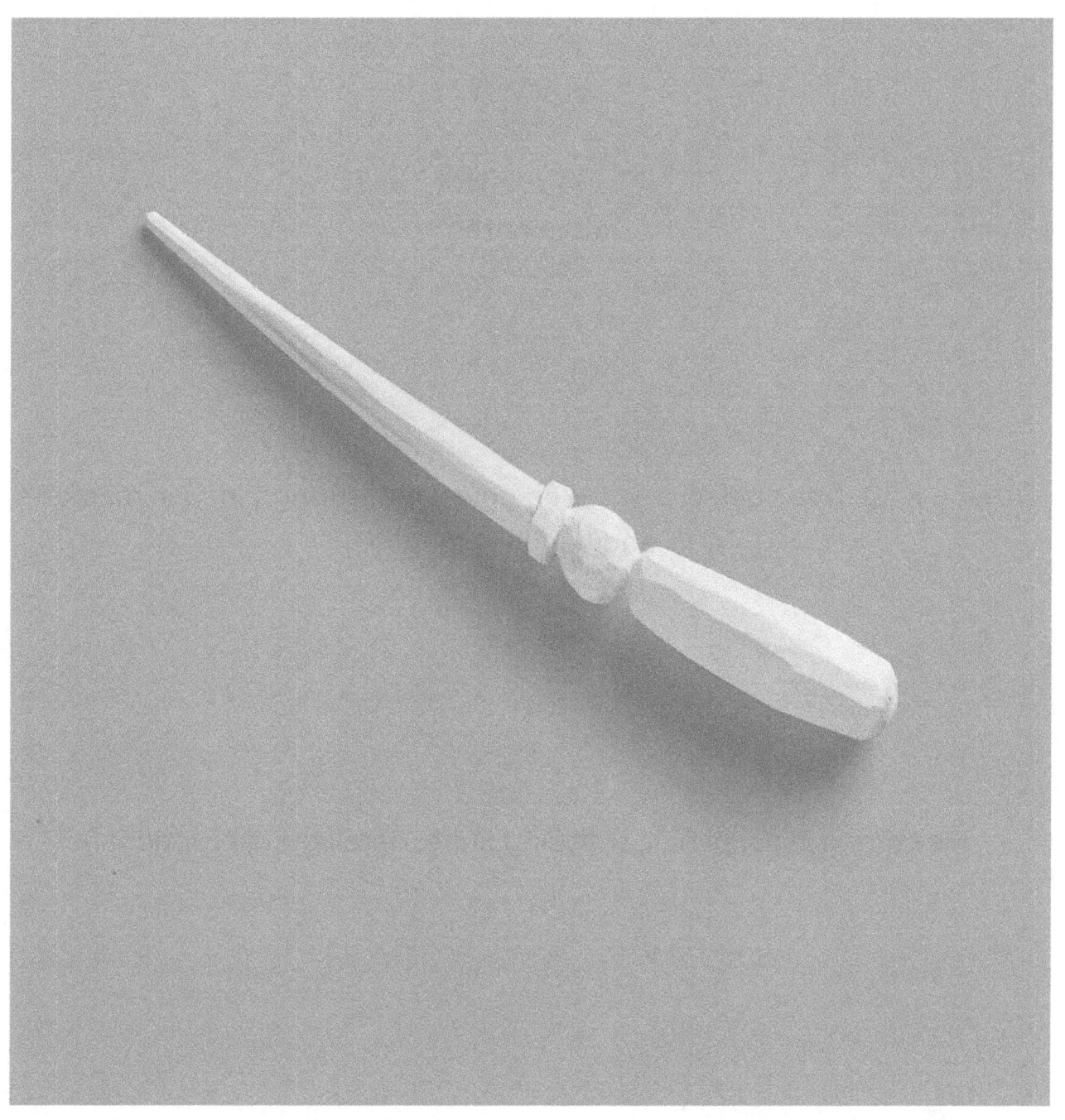

Whittling magic wands is a terrific way to practice several whittling techniques, and they make better gifts than sampler sticks. Feel free to decorate with detail gouges.

START-TO-FINISH TIME:
45 minutes

WOOD DIMENSIONS:
Either a knot-free stick or a wooden dowel measuring 1 inch in diameter and 8 inches long

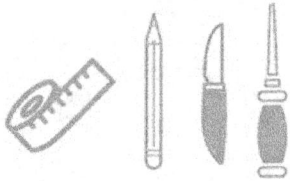

SUPPLIES:
Measuring tape, pencil, whittling knife, detail gouge (optional)

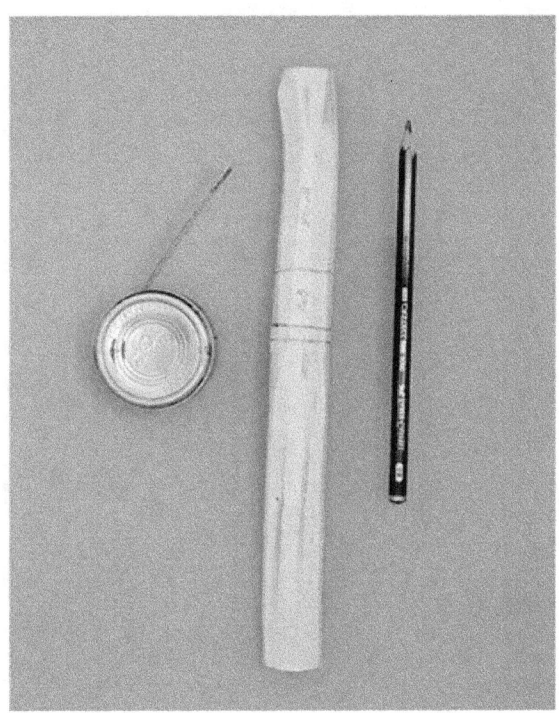

1. Measure and mark the handle. Wrap your hand around one end of the stick and draw a line around the stick at the edge of your hand. Draw a second line around the stick 1 inch higher up, and a third line ¼ inch above that. For example, if your hand is 4 inches wide, you will have three lines at the 4-inch, 5-inch, and 5¼-inch marks.

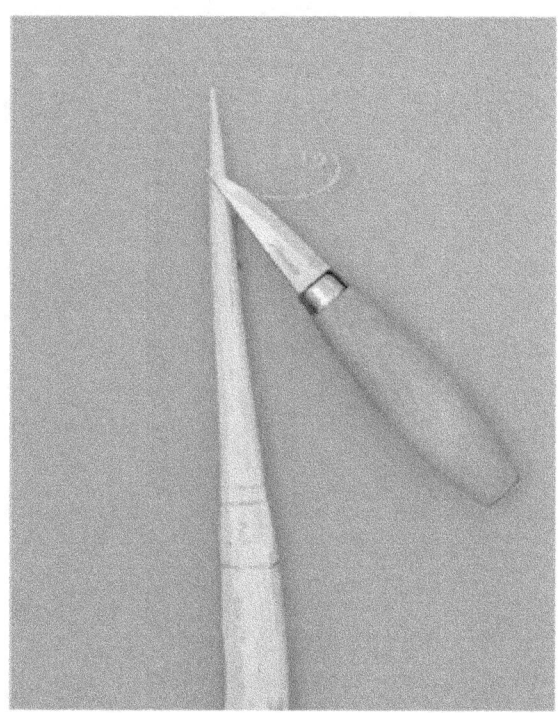

2. Taper the wand. Begin by using the straight cut to carve long, thin shavings starting at the topmost handle line. Rotate the stick with each cut to achieve a consistent, straight tapered wand. Clean up any inconsistencies with a controlled push cut.

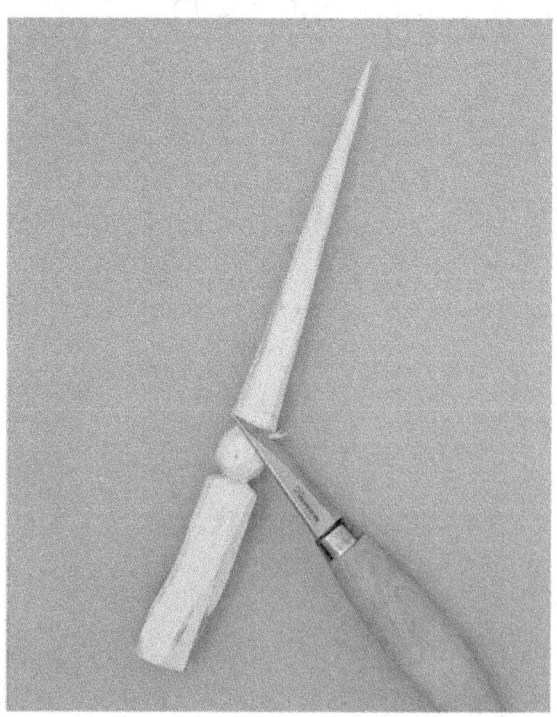

3. Carve a ball between the handle and wand tip. Using the ball technique, carve a ball in the 1-inch section drawn on the wand in step 1. Clean up the edges of the ball with a stop cut on either side, wrapping around the wand. Carve each end of the ball consistently by rotating the stick with each cut.

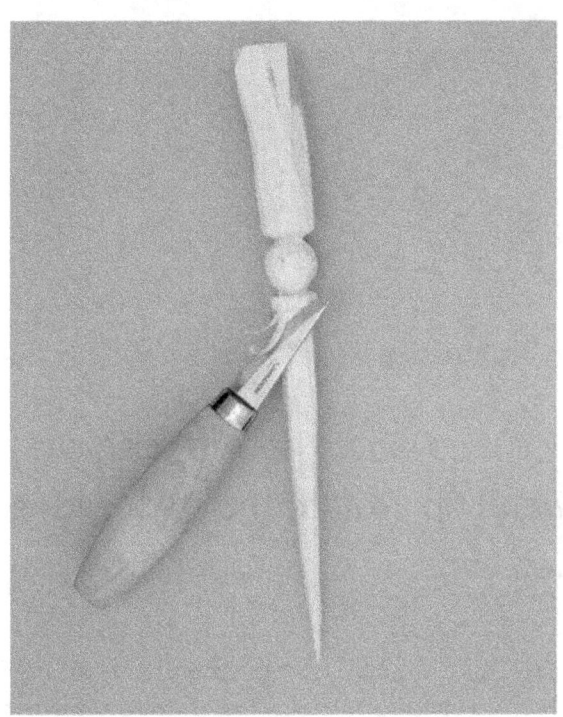

4. Whittle a shoulder between the ball and the tip. Carve a shoulder in the intersection between the wand tip and handle using the stop cut. The topmost line will be the location of the 90-degree cut. Carve toward the 90-degree cut from the wand side to make a distinct edge between your handle and wand tip.

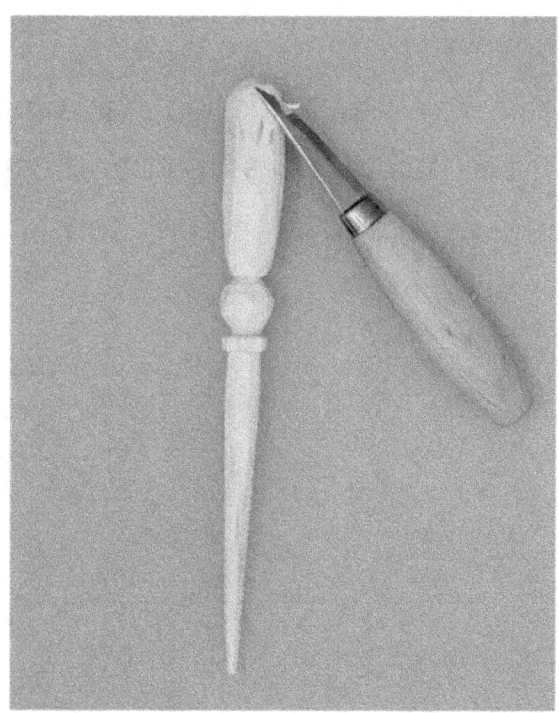

5. Round both ends of the wand. Use the push cut to round the back of the handle and the wand tip. Rotate the stick with each push cut to ensure evenly rounded ends.

> **TECHNIQUE TIP:** Tapering requires particular care and attention. Slow down and notice where thin and thick spots arise after a few passes. Adjust your pressure on the blade accordingly.

Hairpin

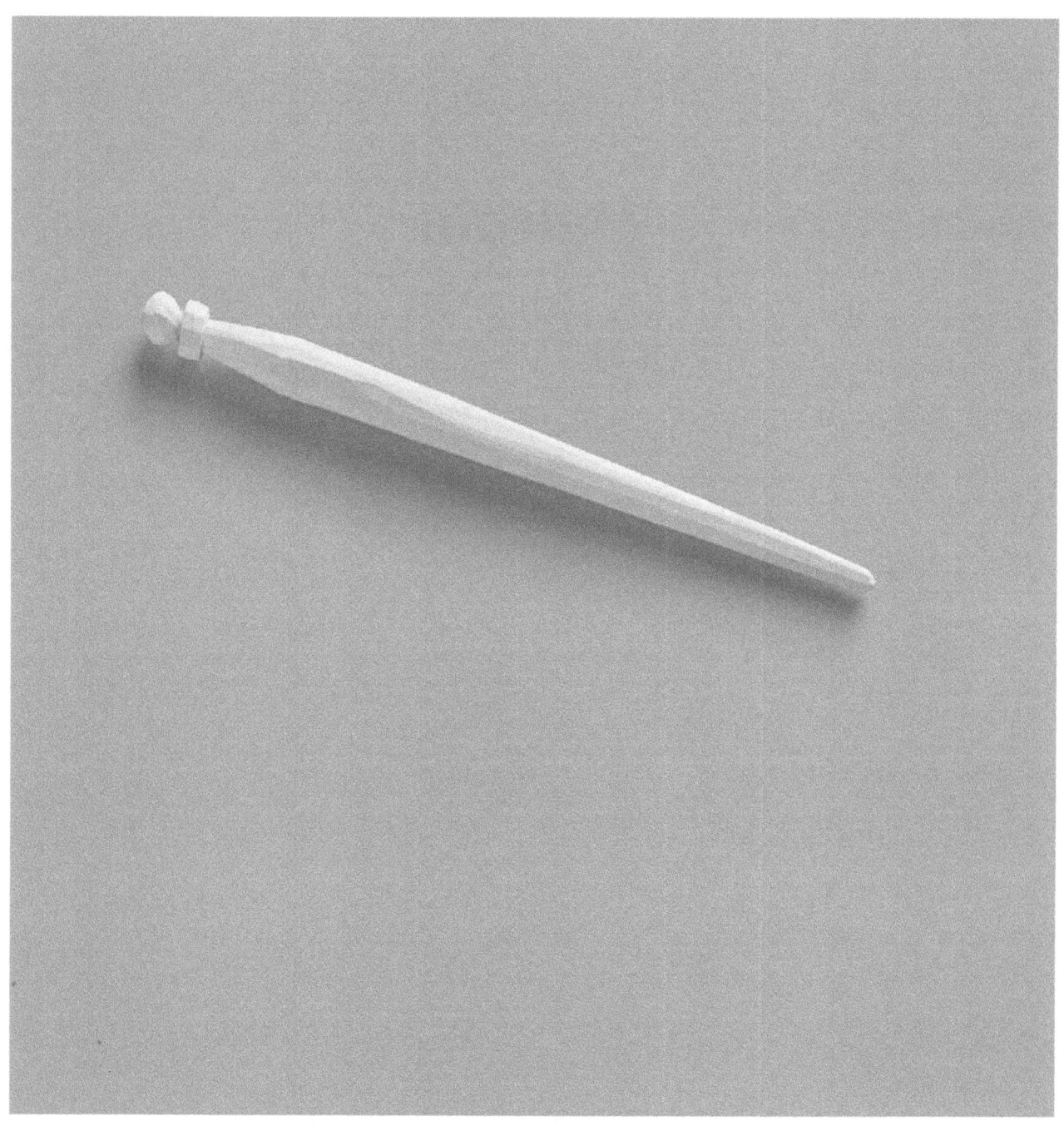

This simple hairpin makes an elegant gift and is a great introduction to decorative carving. This project is easy to repeat with different wood types.

START-TO-FINISH TIME:
45 minutes

WOOD DIMENSIONS:
A dowel or knot-free stick measuring 8 inches long and ½ inch in diameter

SUPPLIES:
Whittling knife, measuring tape, pencil

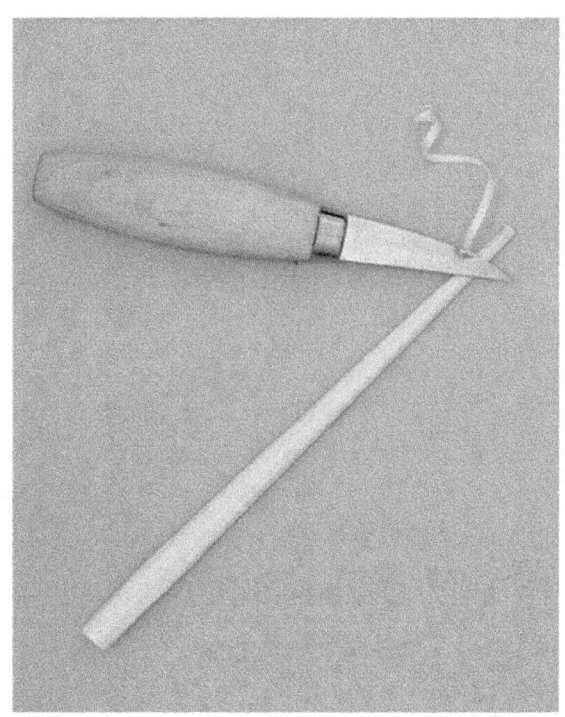

1. Taper the hairpin. Use the straight cut to taper the stick gradually. Rotate the stick with each cut to achieve an even, straight taper. Use the push cut to clean up any inconsistencies. Take care to carve the thin end with shallow cuts to avoid shortening the stick.

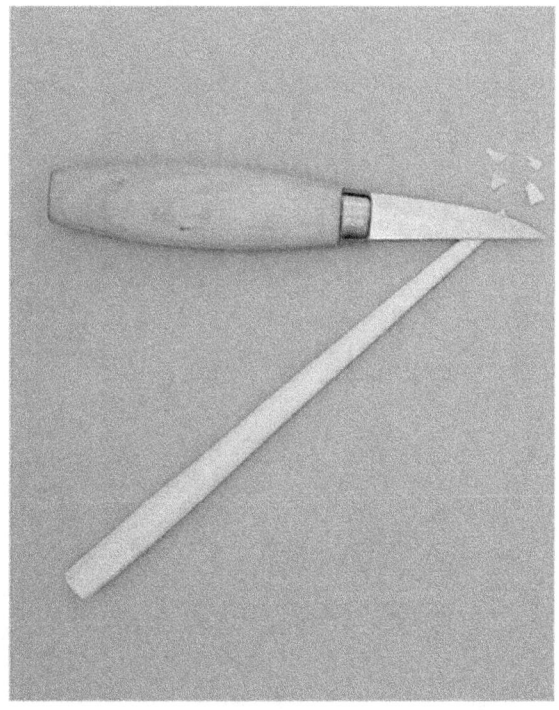

2. Whittle the bottom into a rounded point. Using the push cut, carefully whittle the bottom of the tapered end of the stick into a rounded point. Rotate the stick after each cut to keep the point consistent and centered.

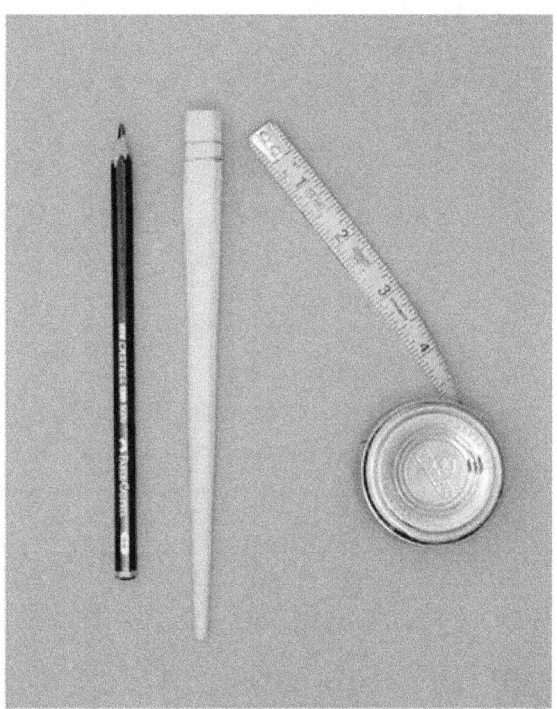

3. Mark the finial. The finial will be a ball resting on a flattened disk on the top of the hairpin. Draw two pencil lines around the stick, ½ inch down from the wide top and ¼ inch below that.

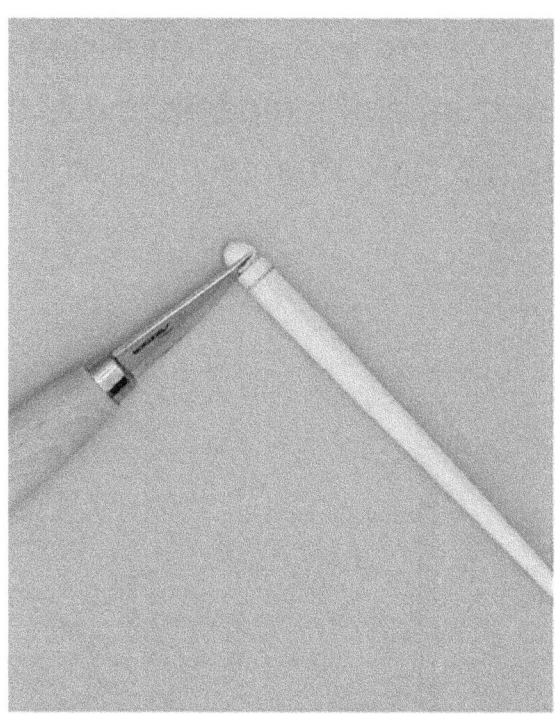

4. Whittle the ball finial. Use the ball cut to whittle the finial in the section between the topmost pencil line and the top edge of the stick. Because there is no wood to hold onto above the ball, use the paring cut to carve the bottom half of the ball.

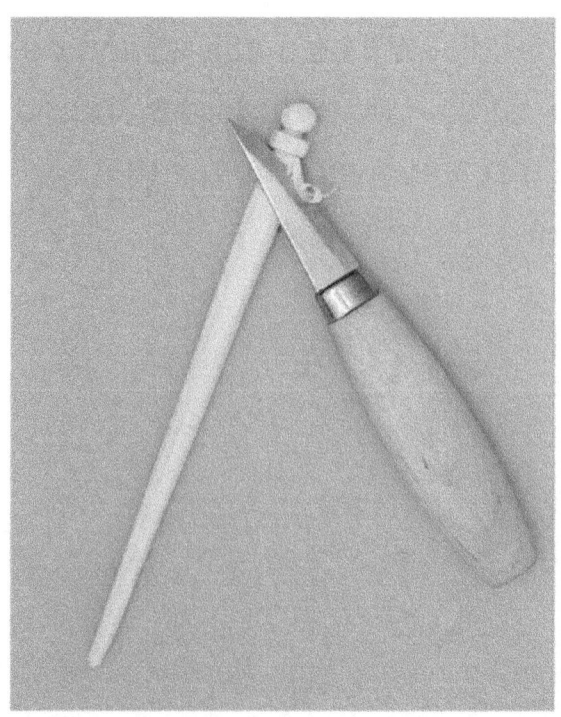

5. Carve the disk. Use the stop cut to carve the disk below the ball. Carve the 90-degree cut into the second pencil line. Carve toward the cut from about 1 inch below it, rotating after each cut to maintain evenness.

> MIX IT UP TIP: As you explore different figure carving shapes later in this book, try returning to this project and whittling more complex finials like bears, leaves, and foxes.

Leaf Pendant

This quick, decorative project offers practice with detail gouges, specifically the v-gouge. It can be used as a pendant, keychain, or earrings.

START-TO-FINISH TIME:
30 minutes

WOOD DIMENSIONS:
A squared piece of basswood measuring 5 inches long, 1 inch wide, and ¼ inch thick

SUPPLIES:
Measuring tape, pencil, whittling knife, detail gouge, saw

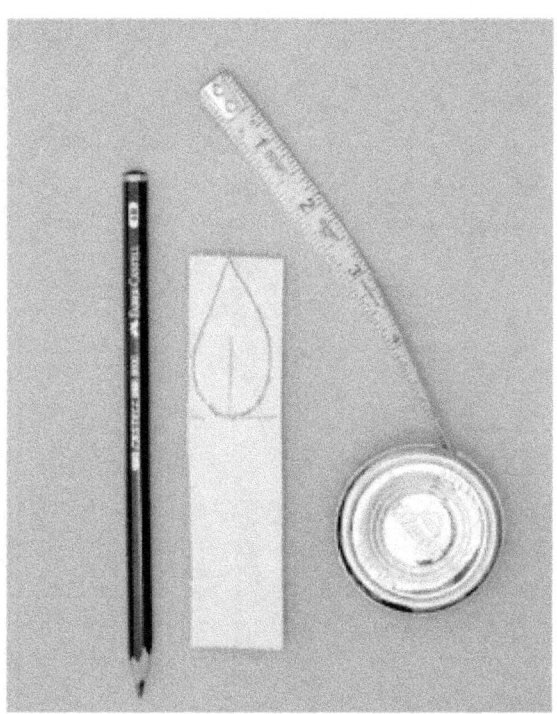

1. Draw the leaf. Begin by marking a line widthwise across the piece of wood 2 inches down from the top to denote the leaf section. In this section, draw a vertical centerline. Then, draw a teardrop that fills the top section of the wood, with the rounded base at the bottom and the pointed tip at the top.

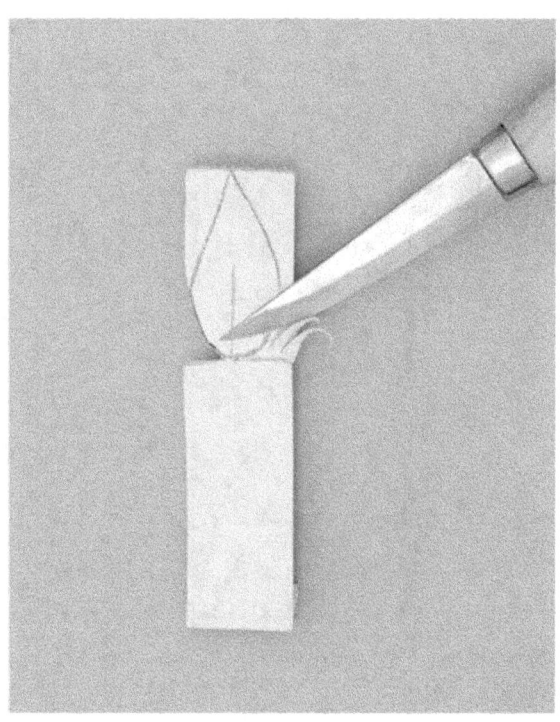

2. Shape the bottom of the leaf. Use a stop cut and paring cut to shape the bottom of the leaf, with the widthwise pencil line as the 90-degree cut. Continue the cut until a ¼-inch piece of wood is holding the leaf to the waste wood.

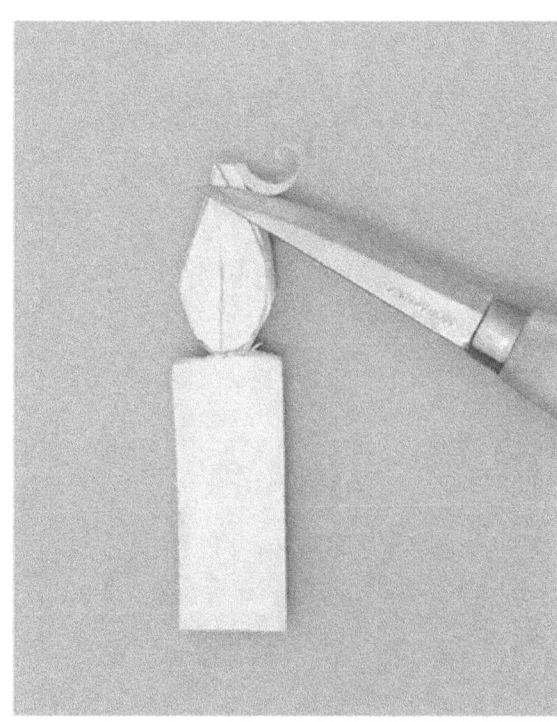

3. Shape the top of the leaf. Use the push cut to whittle the pointed tip of the leaf. Begin at the widest point of the leaf and move forward with each pass until you reach the pencil line.

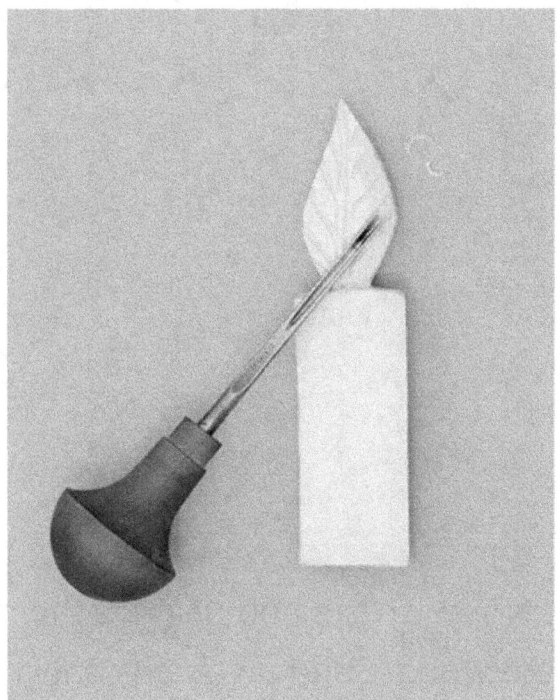

4. Whittle the veins of the leaf. Use the v-gouge to whittle a vein along the centerline. Then, begin at the base of the leaf at the center vein and carve a line out to the edge of the leaf. Repeat four to five more times up each side of the leaf.

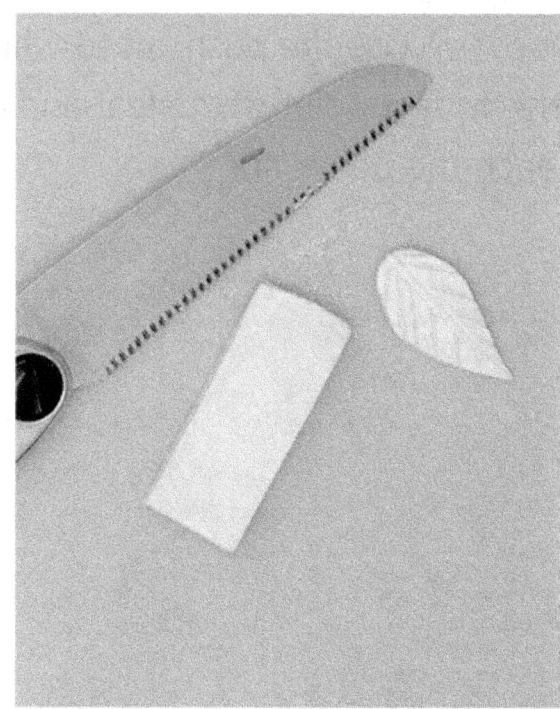

5. Separate the leaf from the waste wood. Anchor the bottom half of the wood firmly on a work surface and use the saw to carefully separate the leaf from the waste wood. Sand away any saw marks.

> **TECHNIQUE TIP:** Like the toggles, you can carve multiple leaves from one piece of wood. Simply add 2 inches to the length for each additional leaf.

Whittled Trees

These little evergreen trees make wonderful holiday decorations and are a great way to understand wood grain. Try painting them green for a realistic look.

START-TO-FINISH TIME:
30 minutes

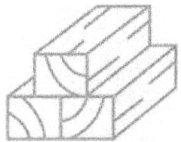

WOOD DIMENSIONS:
Either a knot-free stick or a wooden dowel measuring 6 inches long and ½ inch in diameter

SUPPLIES:
Pencil, whittling knife, saw

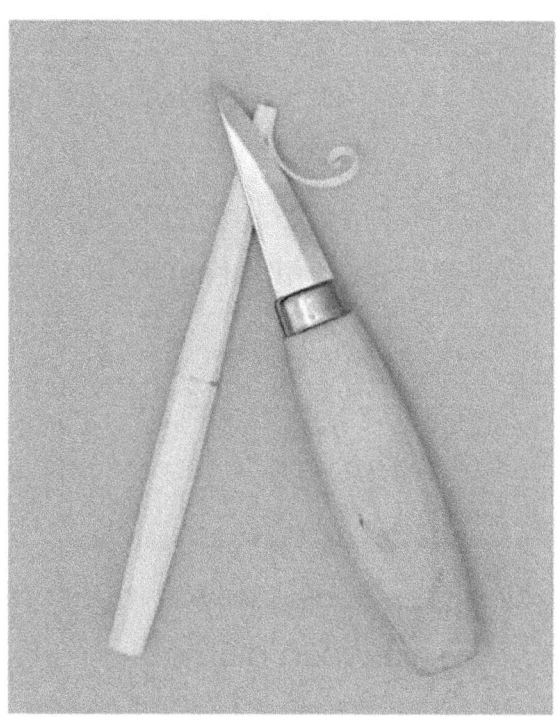

1. Taper the stick. Draw a pencil line around the stick halfway up the length. Use the straight cut to taper the stick beginning at the pencil line and cutting all the way to the end of the wood. Rotate the stick with each pass to maintain consistency.

2. Whittle the top of the tree into a point. Use the push cut to whittle the top of the tree into a point. Rotate the stick with each cut to ensure the point is even and centered.

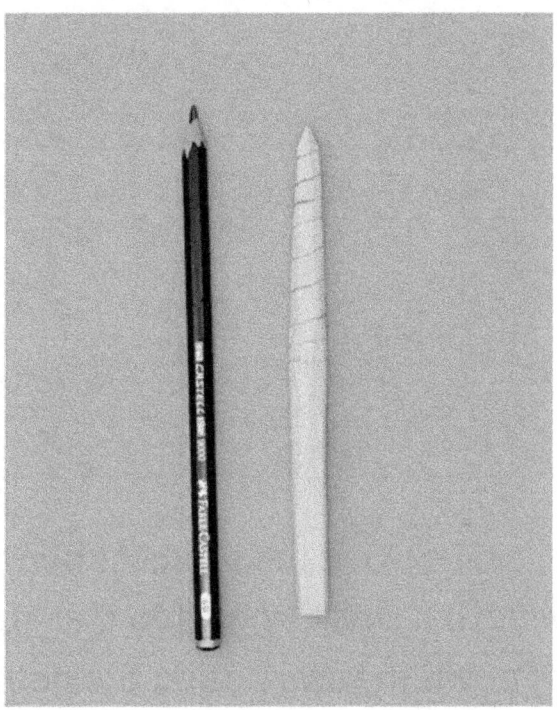

3. Draw a descending spiral. With your pencil, begin at the base of the whittled point and draw a swirled line wrapping down and around the tapered stick. The tighter the swirl, the more rows of branches your tree will have.

4. Whittle the branches. Begin at the topmost pencil line and use the push cut to carefully carve a small woodchip that stays attached. Continue this process down the swirl, using the pencil line as the start of the cut and ending just below the row of cuts above.

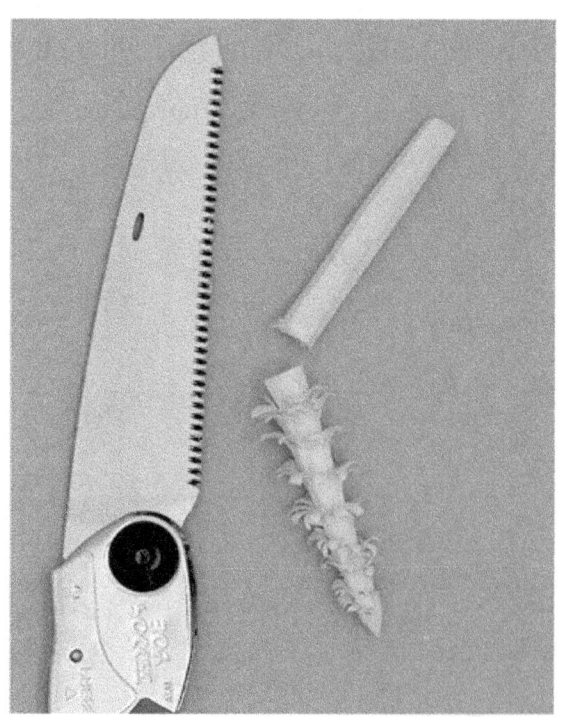

5. Separate the tree. First, anchor the bottom of the stick on a work surface and gently saw apart the tree from the rest of the stick. Since the tree is delicate, make sure it doesn't fall too far once it is separated.

> **TECHNIQUE TIP:** The controlled push cut in this project can be difficult to achieve at first. Try practicing on a piece of scrap wood before whittling the tree branches.

Simple Fishing Handline

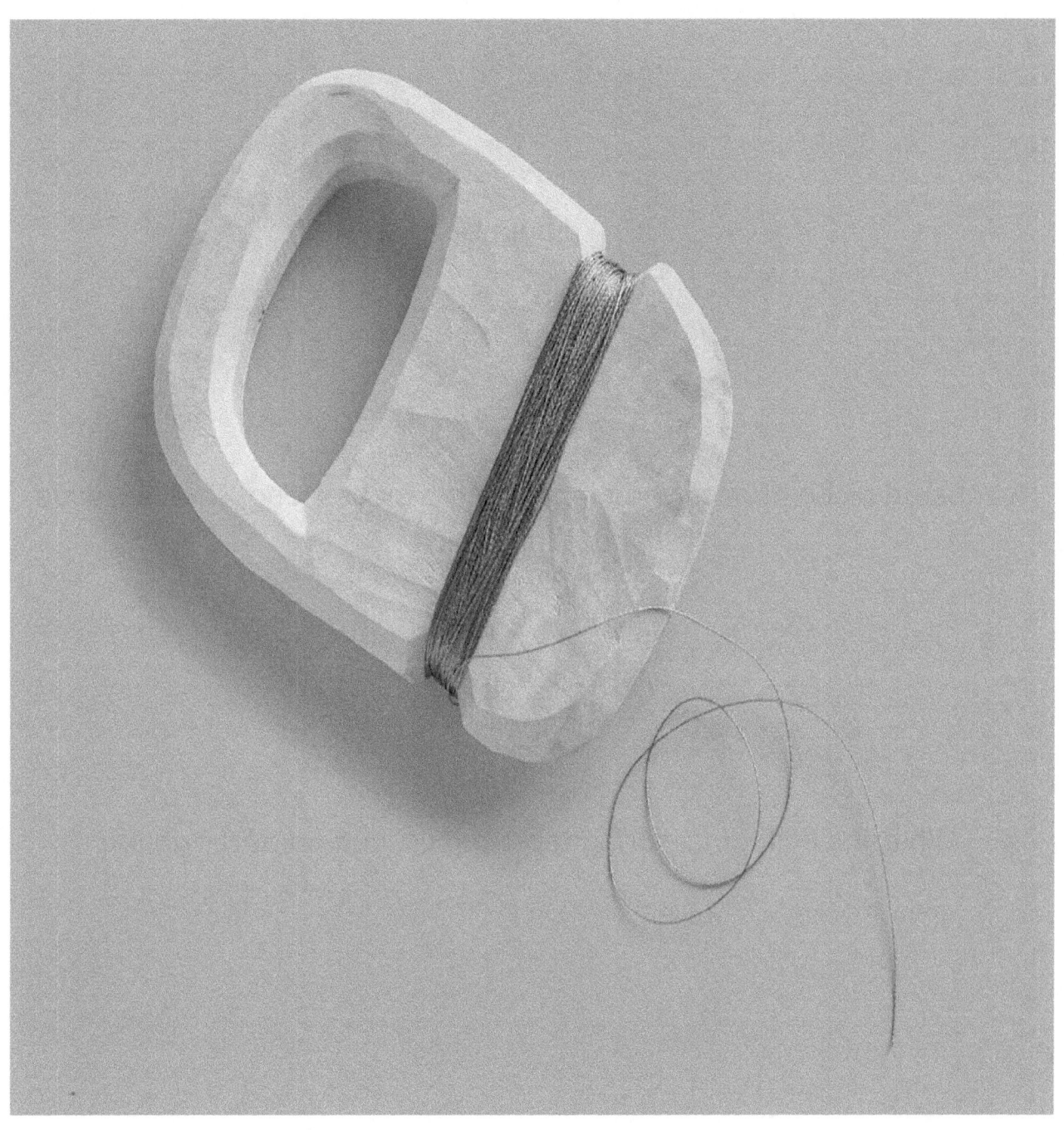

A fishing handline is a portable fishing line that easily fits in a backpack. It's a great project to show off several introductory techniques.

START-TO-FINISH TIME:
1 hour

WOOD DIMENSIONS:
A squared piece of basswood measuring 5 inches long, 4 inches wide, and ½ inch thick

SUPPLIES:
Whittling knife, measuring tape, pencil, curved detail gouge

1. Round the corners. Use the push cut to round each corner of the piece of wood. Begin by thinning the front and back of each corner and then round the side profile. See the technique tip for making the corners consistent.

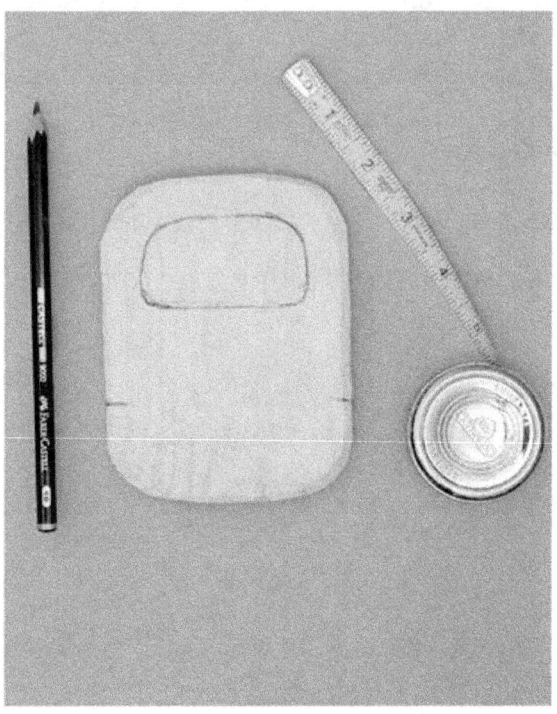

2. Mark the handle and notch locations. With the grain oriented vertically, anchor your hand in order to trace a consistent line that is set about ½ inch from the top edge, running parallel and ending 1½ inches down either side. Then, draw a line to connect the bottom points, thus marking the handle area. Measure 1½ inches up from the bottom on either side for the notch marks.

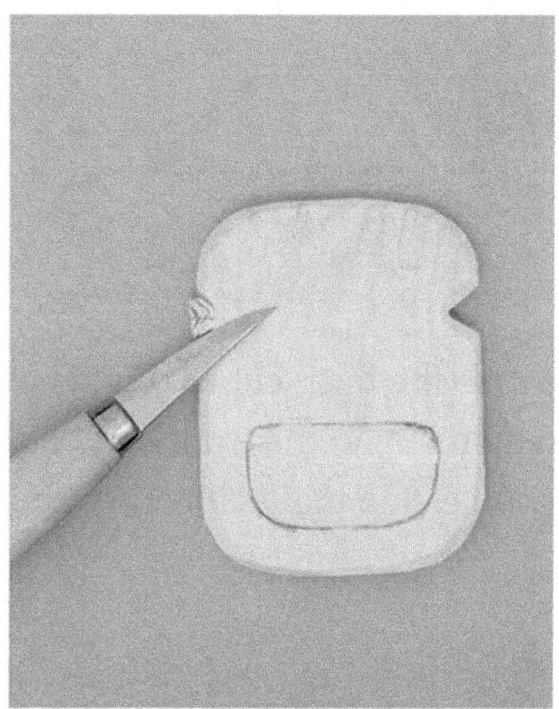

3. Whittle the notch for the fishing line. Use the v-cut to whittle a notch where the fishing line will wrap around the handline, using the notch marks for reference. Continue until each notch is ½ inch deep.

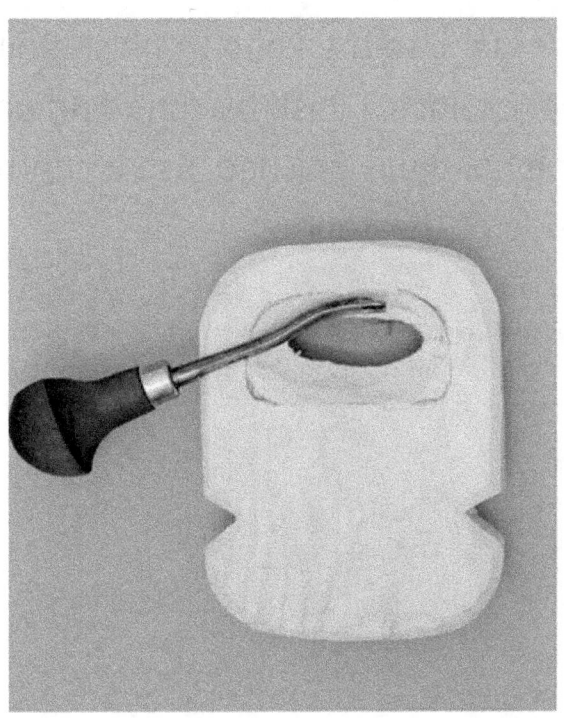

4. Carve out the handle hole. Use your curved detail gouge to carve out the handle area you drew in step 2. Continue until you carve through to the other side and the hole is large enough for your whittling knife to fit through.

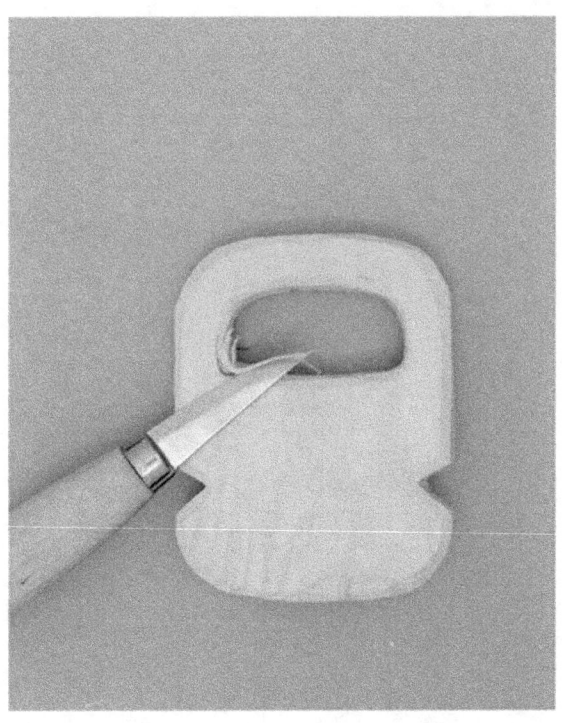

5. Shape the handle hole. Use the knife to finish hollowing out the handle hole to the pencil lines. Finish by rounding any hard corners. Once the inside of the handle is finished, use a controlled push cut to smooth out the outside of the handle.

> **TECHNIQUE TIP:** Make consistent corners with a traceable template. Begin with a 1-inch square piece of paper. Fold it in half widthwise and lengthwise, and then round the unfolded corner with scissors.

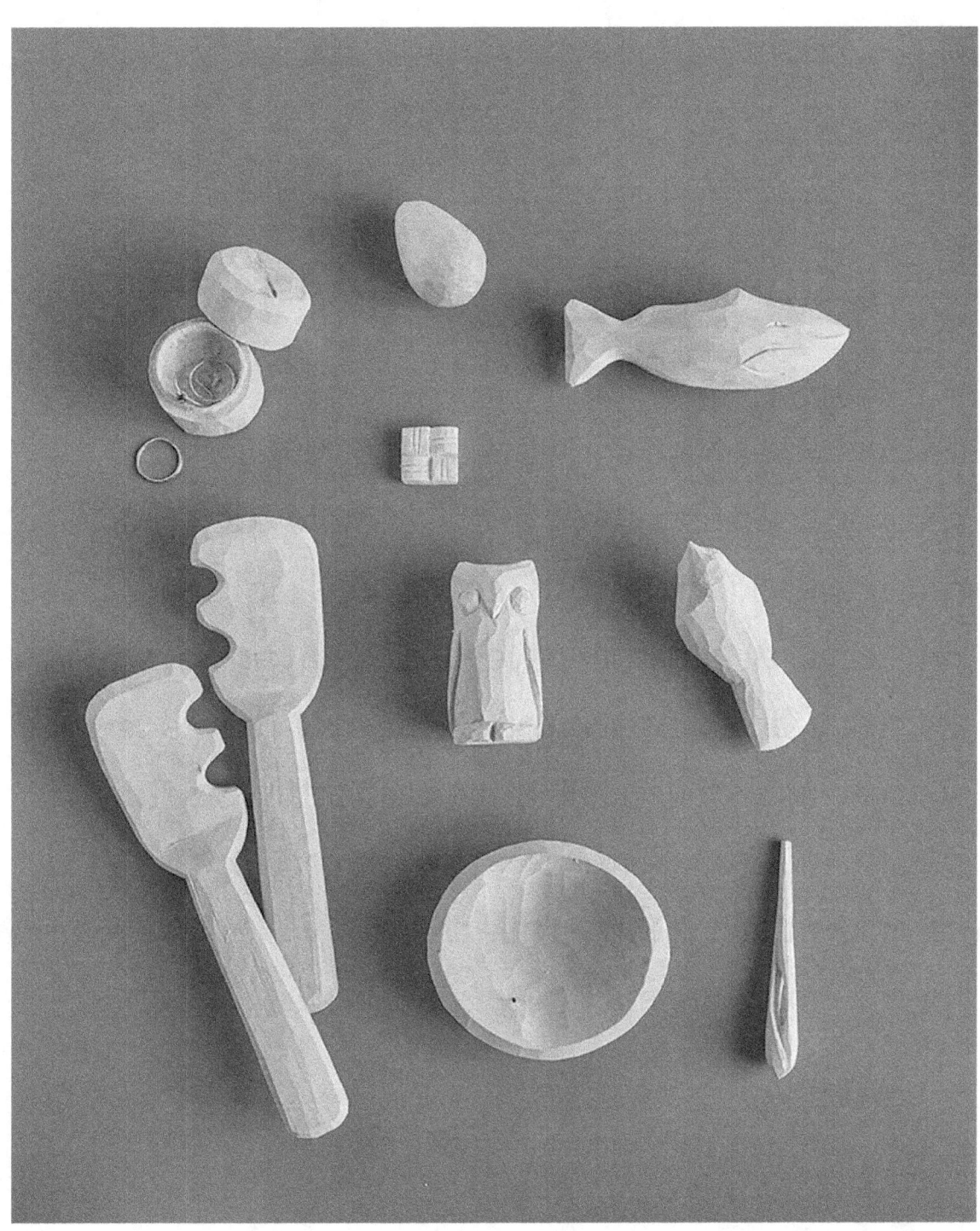

THREE

SKILL-BUILDING PROJECTS

This chapter builds upon the core techniques from chapter 2 and uses them to create more complex projects designed to strengthen your skills. Some of the projects in this chapter have more detailed steps so you will not need a pattern. You will need to draw a few simple shapes, but none of the elements have strict placements, so feel free to get creative! Once you complete the projects in this chapter, you will be ready for the more intricate projects in chapter 4.

Whittled Egg

Small Salt Bowl

Woven-Knot Pendant

Spiral Ornament

Comfort Bird

Salad Servers

Perching Owl

Lidded Box

Whittled Whale

Whittled Egg

This simple egg offers practice with the ball cut and makes a beautiful table decoration. The egg can be sanded smooth and painted or left plain.

START-TO-FINISH TIME:
45 minutes

WOOD DIMENSIONS:
A squared piece of basswood measuring 5 inches long, 1½ inches wide, and 1½ inches thick

SUPPLIES:
Whittling knife, measuring tape, pencil, saw

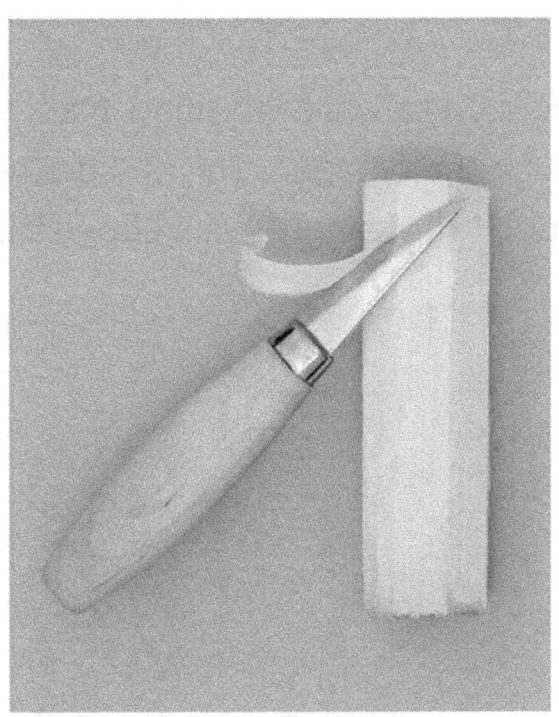

1. Round the vertical corners of the wood block. Use the straight cut to carve off the vertical corners, so the block is an octagon (eight-sided) in cross-section. Starting with a faceted shape, as opposed to a cylinder, is an easier way to achieve a consistent and even egg shape.

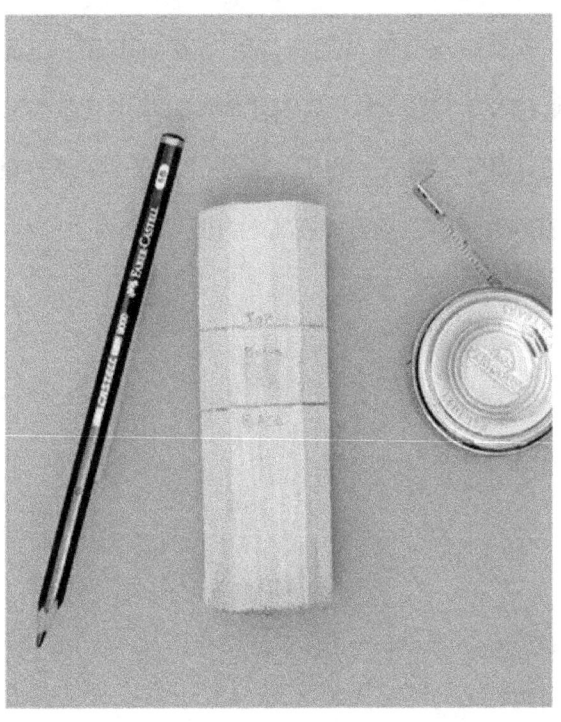

2. Mark the wide point and the bottom of the egg. Half of the length of wood is for you to hold on to while whittling. Mark a line halfway up the block, wrapping around the octagon. This will be the bottom of your egg. Mark the wide point of the egg 1 inch above the first line.

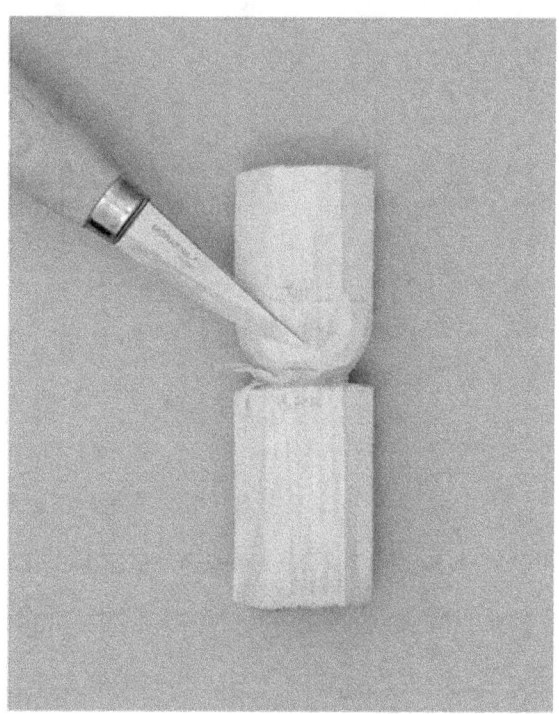

3. Whittle the base of the egg. Use half of a ball cut to whittle the bottom of the egg. Carve the 90-degree cut into the bottom pencil line and use the top pencil line to begin each cut toward it. Continue until the cut is ½ inch deep all the way around.

4. Whittle the top of the egg. Using a push cut, carve the top section of the egg into a rounded, pointed shape. Rotate the block with each pass to ensure that your egg stays centered and even. Use the 8 facets for reference to maintain consistency.

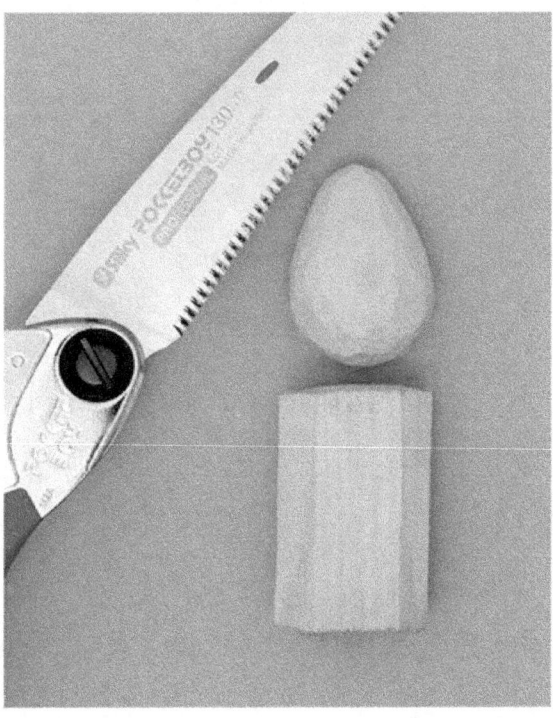

5. Separate the egg from the block. Anchor the squared section of the block to a work surface and carefully separate the egg from the block with a saw. Touch up any saw marks with your whittling knife or sandpaper.

> **PERSONALIZE IT TIP:** Eggs come in many sizes and colors. Try customizing your egg to a bird species by looking up the specifics online and then painting it.

Small Salt Bowl

This shallow salt bowl will teach you the fundamentals of bowl carving in a manageable project suitable for hand tools.

START-TO-FINISH TIME:

1 hour 45 minutes

WOOD DIMENSIONS:

A squared piece of basswood measuring 3 to 4 inches long, 3 to 4 inches wide, and 1 inch thick

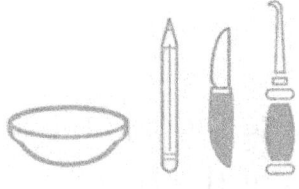

SUPPLIES:

Circular lid for tracing, pencil, whittling knife, curved detail gouge

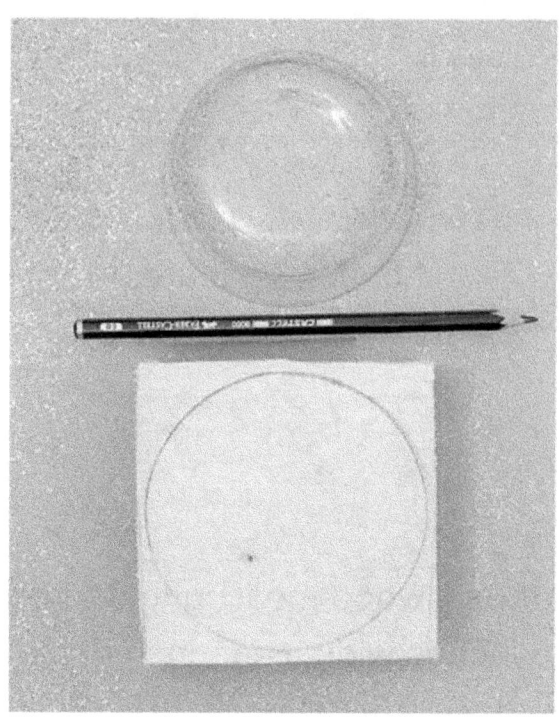

1. Trace the circular template onto the top of the block. Center your circle on the square face of the block, and trace around it. This will be the guideline for the outside of the bowl.

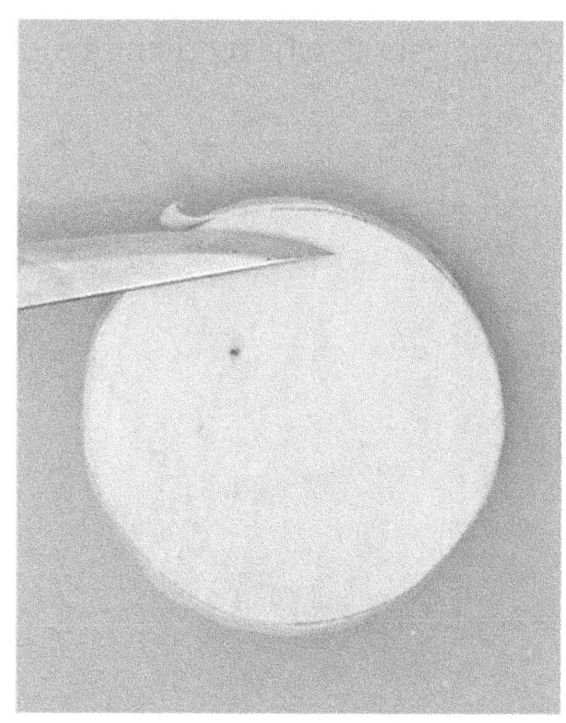

2. Shape the outside of the bowl. Use the push cut and paring cut to shape the outside of the bowl to the pencil lines. Continue until the wood block is an even cylinder.

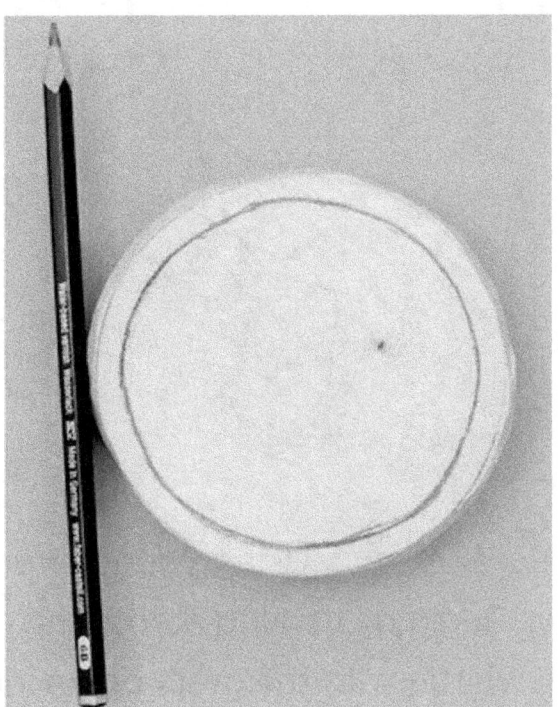

3. Draw the guideline for the inside of the bowl. Anchor your hand on the newly carved edge, and carefully sketch a circle that is set ¼ inch in from the edge. This will be your guideline while whittling the inside.

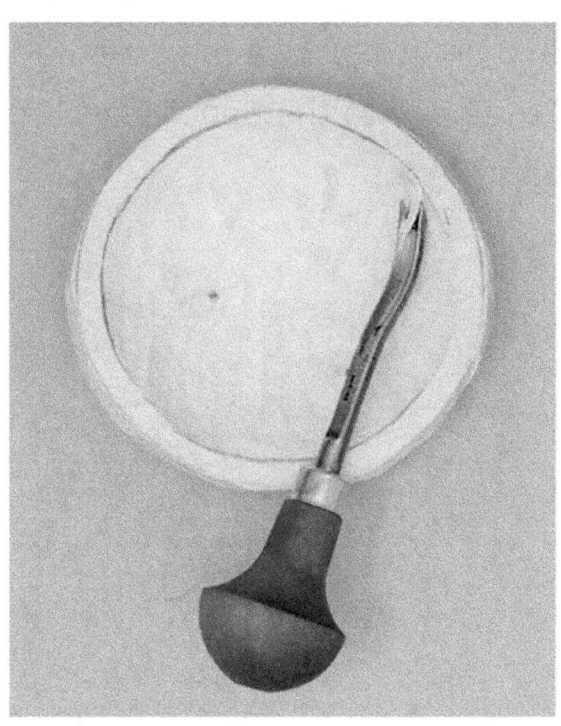

4. Whittle the inside of the bowl. Using your curved gouge, hollow out the inside of the bowl. Begin by carving across the grain for a more aggressive cut. Then, whittle with the grain down into the bowl to smooth and shape it.

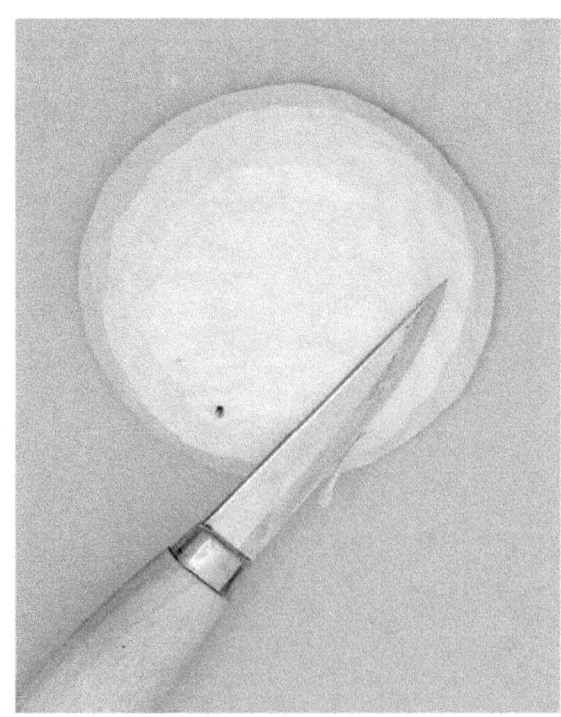

5. Shape the curved outside of the bowl. Using the push cut and paring cut, shape the outside of the bowl. Pinch the walls of the bowl occasionally to test the thickness and avoid carving through the bowl.

> **MIX IT UP TIP:** A 3- to 4-inch diameter bowl is the perfect size for the tools in this book. Try whittling a 5- to 8-inch bowl if you have a larger gouge.

Woven-Knot Pendant

This woven-knot pendant offers great practice for the stop cut on a wide, flat piece of wood. Try sanding the pendant for a polished look.

START-TO-FINISH TIME:
45 minutes

WOOD DIMENSIONS:
A squared piece of basswood measuring 3 inches long, 1 inch wide, and ½ inch thick

SUPPLIES:
Measuring tape, pencil, whittling knife, skew chisel (optional), detail gouge, saw

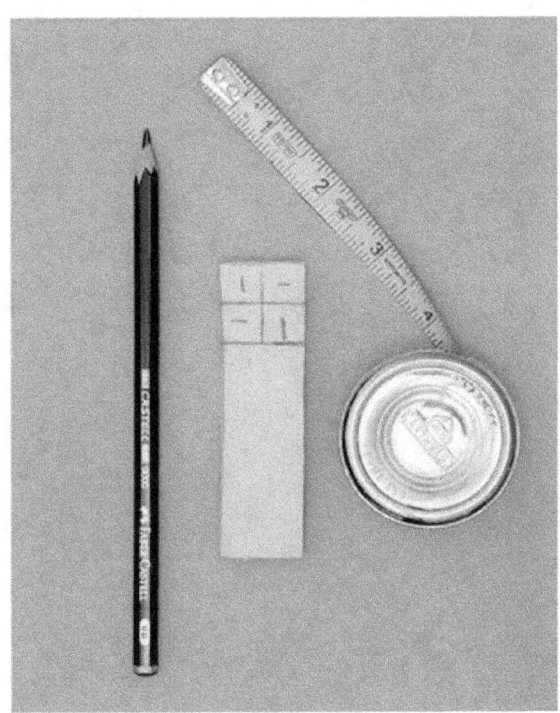

1. Draw the pendant shape and design. Draw a line with a pencil across the 1-inch-wide side of the wood, 1 inch down from the top. Within this 1-inch square, draw a vertical and horizontal centerline to make four quadrants. Draw alternating horizontal and vertical marks in each quadrant.

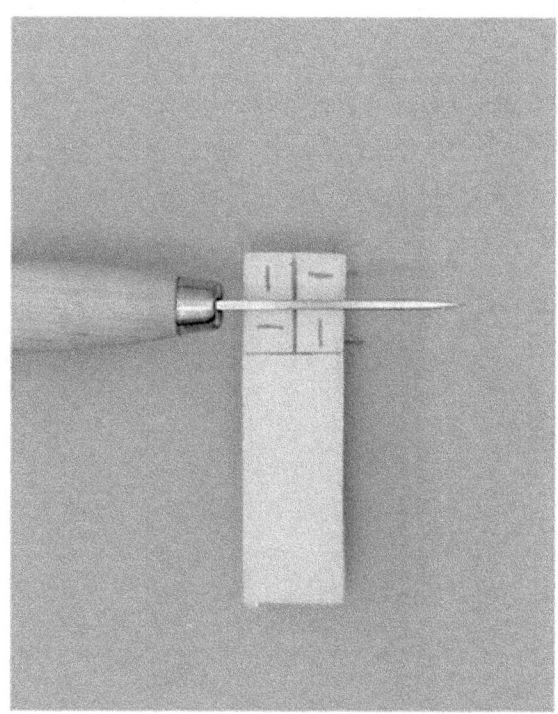

2. Make 90-DEGREE CUTS ALONG THE CENTERLINES. The weave will be whittled with a series of stop cuts. Begin by making a 90-degree cut along each centerline. Take care to carve to the same depth for each cut.

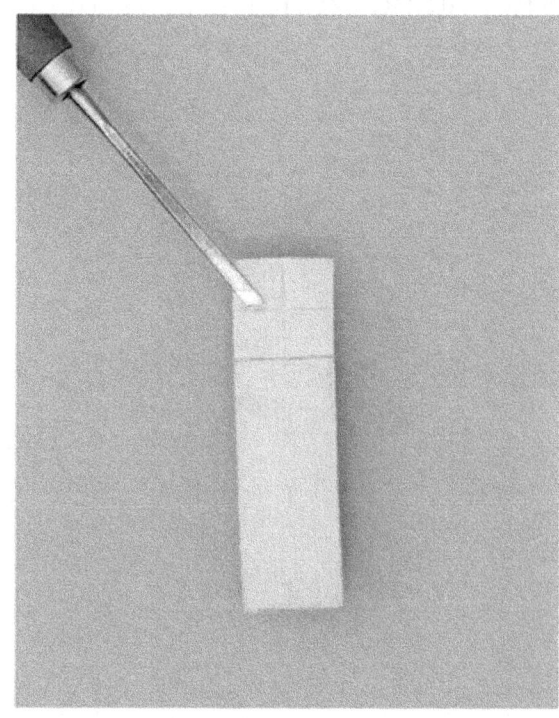

3. Shape the woven design. Using either the tip of your knife or a small skew chisel, carve toward each 90-degree cut. For the horizontally marked quadrants, carve toward the 90-degree cuts on the left and right. On the vertically marked quadrants, carve toward the 90-degree cut above and below.

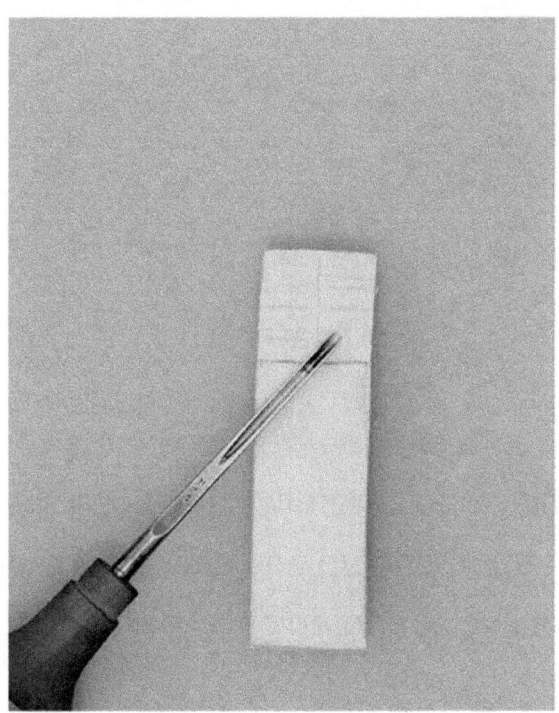

4. Carve the details. With the v-gouge, carve two horizontal lines into each horizontal quadrant and two vertical lines into each vertical quadrant.

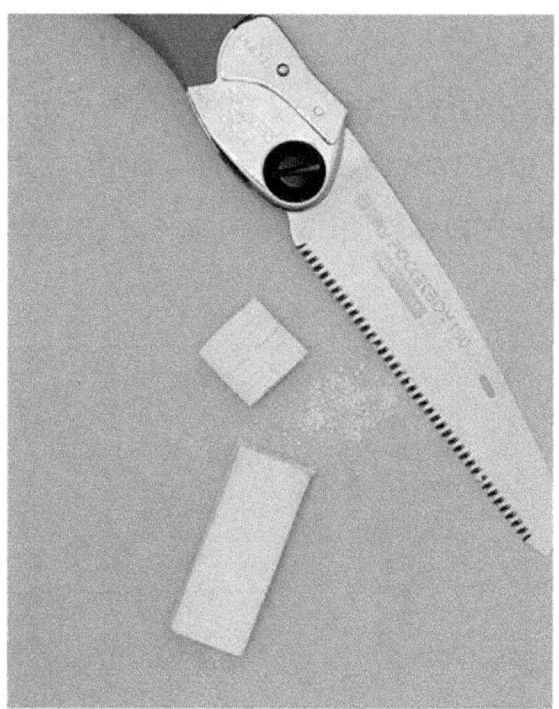

5. Separate the pendant from the rest of the wood. Secure the piece of wood on a work surface and carefully saw along the bottom pencil line to separate the pendant. Clean up any saw marks with sandpaper. Screw in a little metal eyelet and enjoy!

MIX IT UP TIP: This small project is a great opportunity to sample different wood types. Try whittling the pendant out of walnut, cherry, or oak.

Spiral Ornament

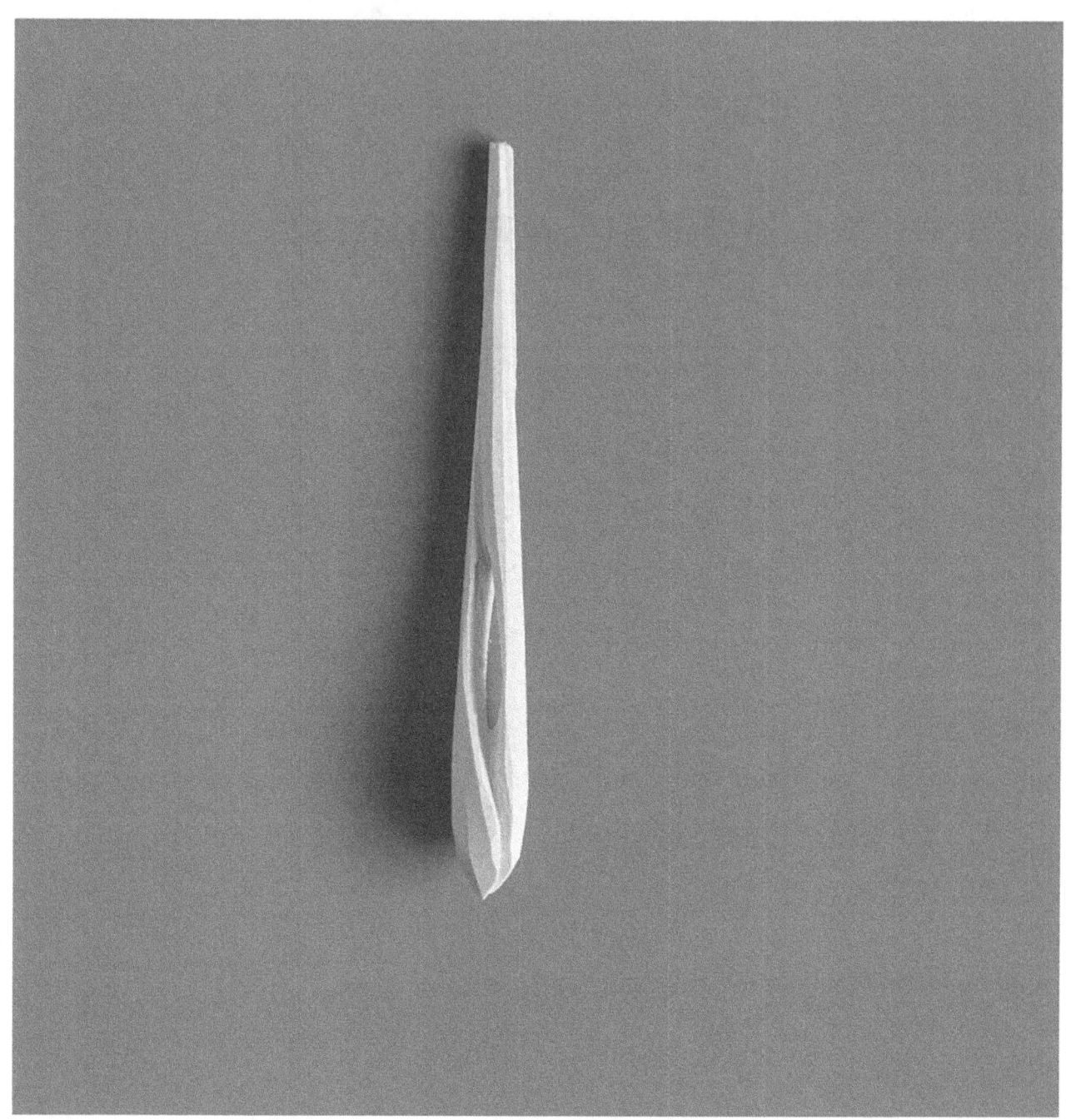

This elongated teardrop ornament, with a double spiral and cut-through center, resembles an icicle and spins beautifully on a holiday tree.

START-TO-FINISH TIME:
1 hour 30 minutes

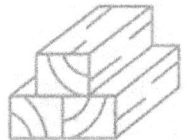

WOOD DIMENSIONS:
A knot-free stick or dowel measuring 8 inches long and ½ inch in diameter

SUPPLIES:
Measuring tape, pencil, whittling knife, detail gouge, saw

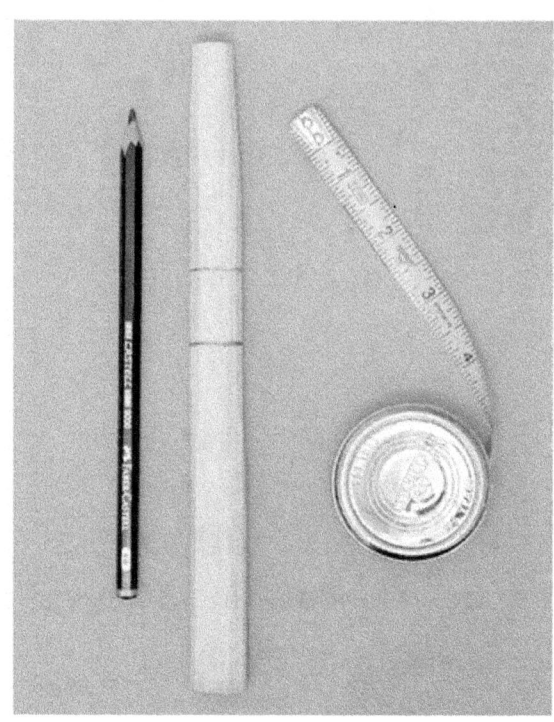

1. Mark the ornament and the wide point. Using your measuring tape and pencil, mark a line around the stick 4 inches down from the top. Mark another line around the stick 1 inch above that for the ornament's wide point.

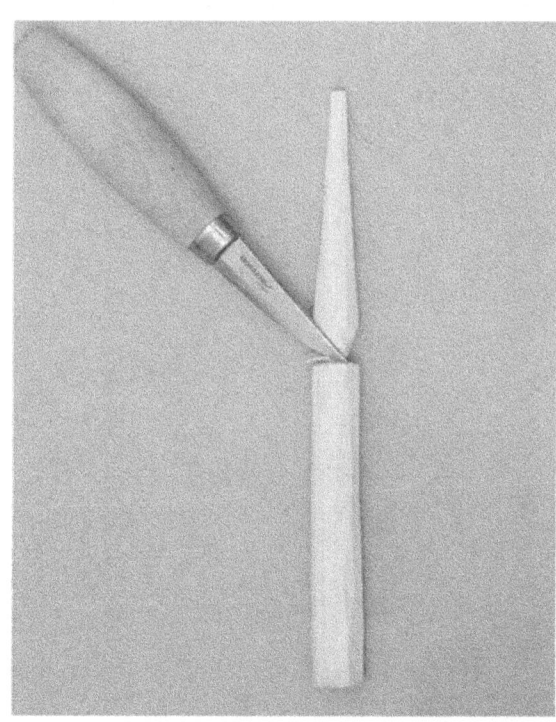

2. Shape the ornament. Use the straight cut to gently taper the top 3 inches of the ornament to a rounded point. Use a half ball cut to round the bottom of the ornament. Make sure to leave at least a ¼-inch connection of the ornament to the waste wood.

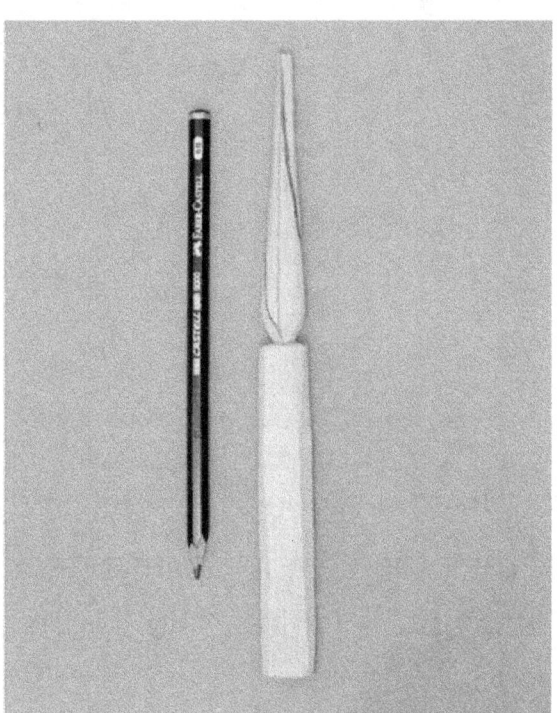

3. Draw the spirals. Draw vertical centerlines on opposite sides of the ornament. Beginning at the top of the first line, draw a line spiraling down the ornament that lands at the bottom of the opposite line. Repeat for the second line, creating two parallel spirals.

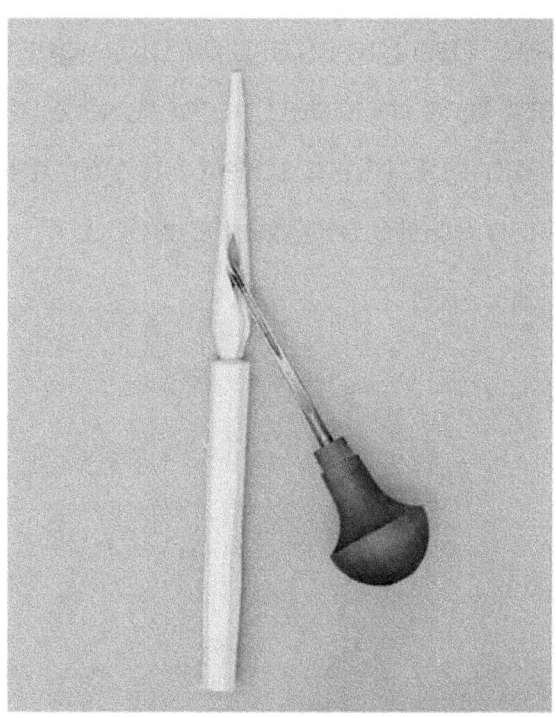

4. Whittle the spirals. Use the v-gouge to whittle the spirals. Carve through the center of the ornament in the mid-section, making a hole about ½ inch long. Clean up the whittled hole with a skew chisel or the tip of your knife.

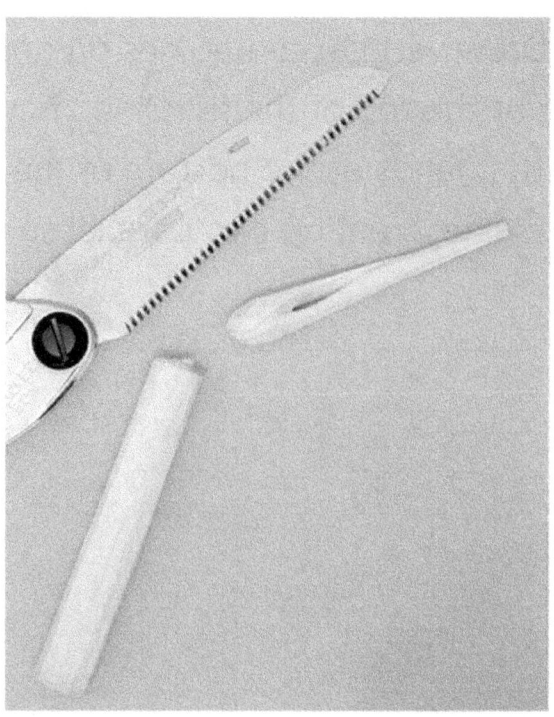

5. Separate the ornament. Secure the waste wood on the work surface and gently saw the ornament free at the base. Make sure the ornament doesn't fall far off the work surface. Clean up any saw marks with a push cut.

PERSONALIZE IT TIP: For a more festive look, try sanding and painting these ornaments, using acrylic or interference paint for an iridescent shine.

Comfort Bird

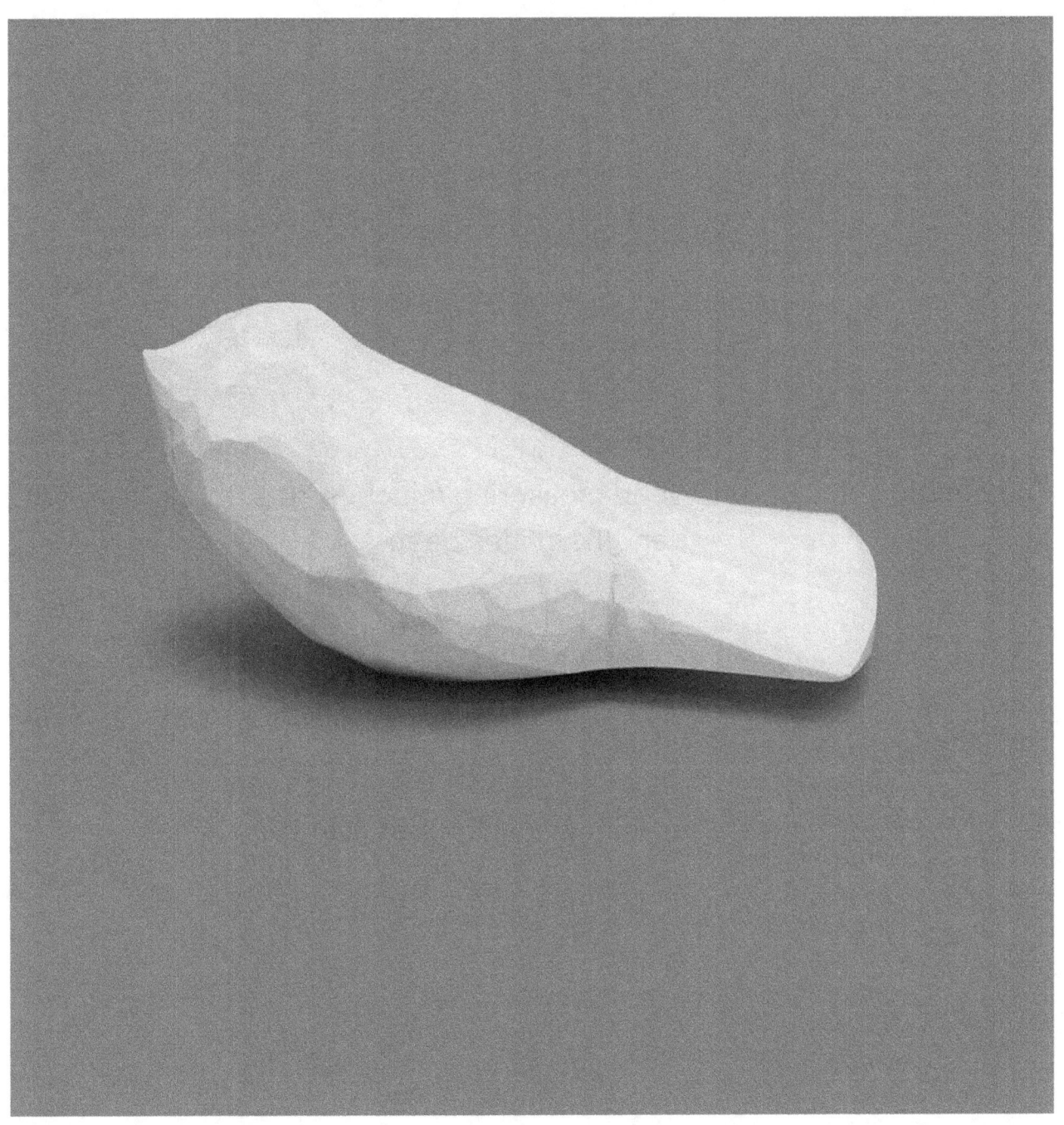

Comfort birds are traditionally gifted to loved ones who are having a tough time. They are designed to fit perfectly in your palm.

START-TO-FINISH TIME:
1 hour 30 minutes

WOOD DIMENSIONS:
A squared piece of basswood measuring 4 inches long, 1½ inches wide, and 1½ inches deep

SUPPLIES:
Whittling knife, measuring tape, pencil

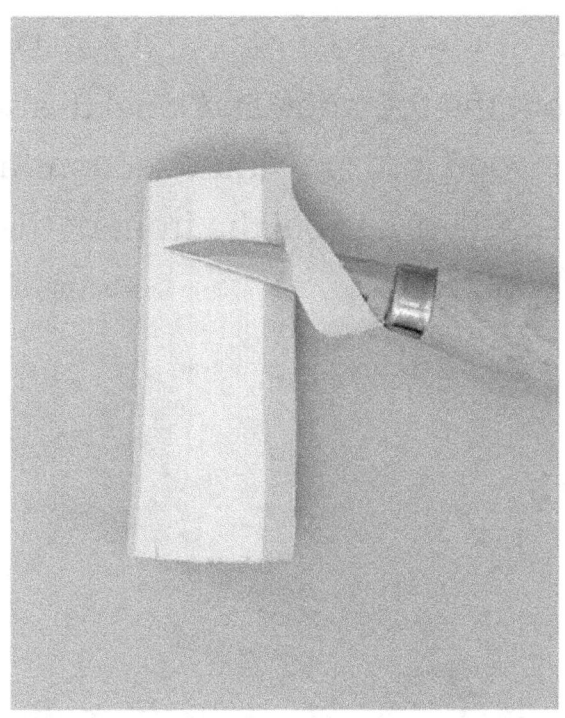

1. Round the vertical edges. Use the paring cut and push cut to round the vertical corners so that the wood block is an octagon (eight-sided) in the cross-section. Continue until all facets are equal in width.

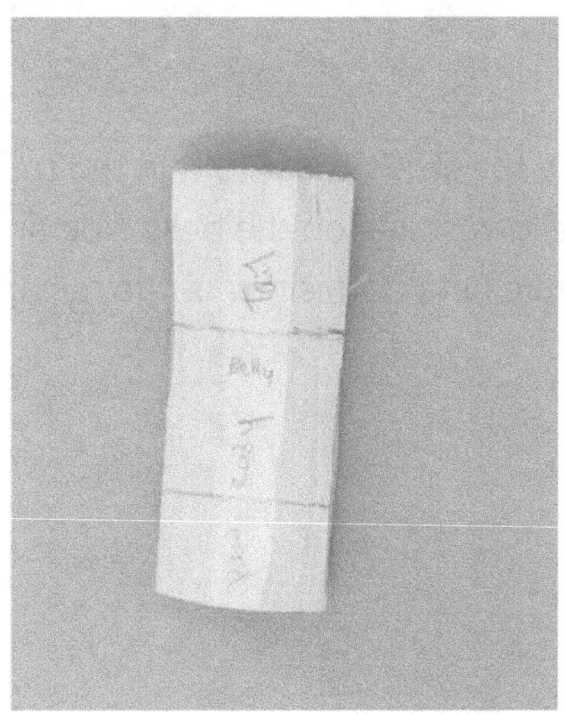

2. Mark the locations of the head, body, and tail. Draw a line around the block 1 inch down from the top edge and label this section "head." Then, divide the remaining wood into two equal sections and label them "body" and "tail," respectively. Label the front of the block "belly" and the back of the block "back."

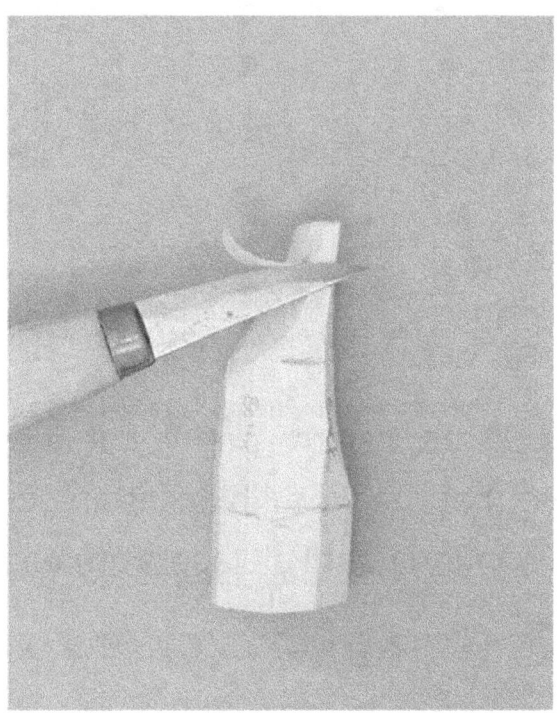

3. Shape the tail. Use the straight cut to thin the top and bottom of the tail, beginning at the lowest line on the belly side and the upper line on the back side. Continue until both sides of the tail are parallel and ¼ inch thick at the base.

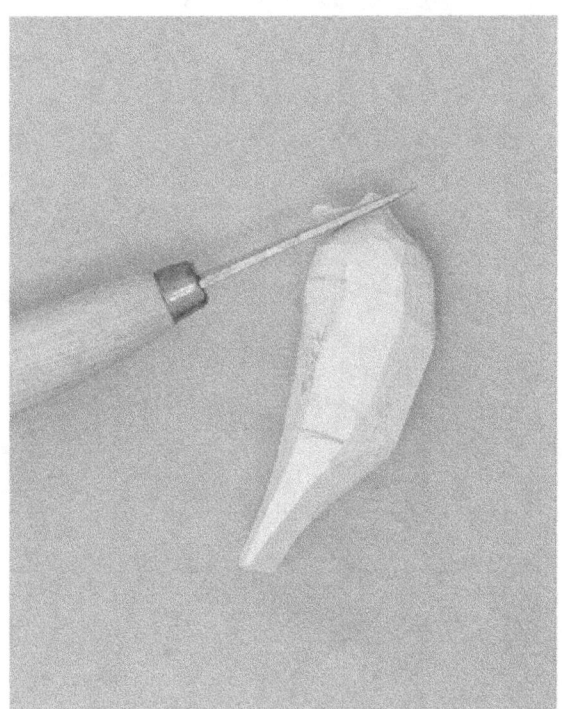

4. Whittle the head. Begin on the belly side at the topmost line and use the push cut to round the head upward, ending ¼ inch from the side labeled "back." Then, continue with the push cut around the sides of the head, leaving a conical section of wood approximately ¼ inch long for the beak.

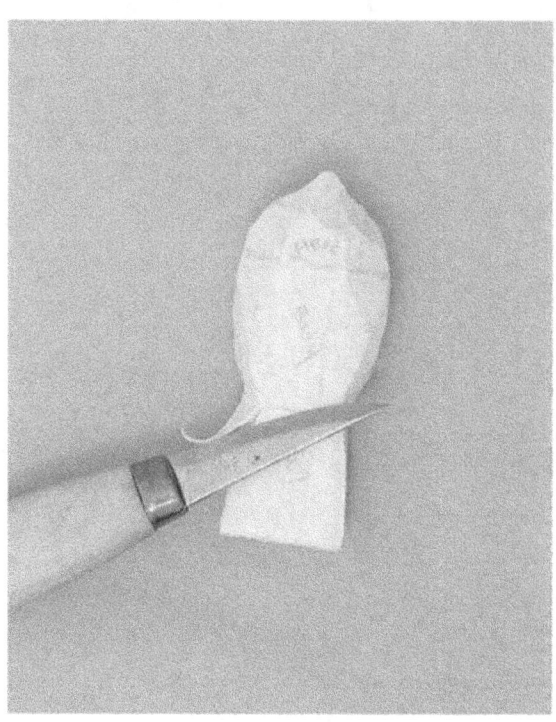

5. Shape the intersection between the body and the tail. Use the v-cut on the sides of the block to shape the intersection between the tail and the body. Round the body-half of the cut and taper the tail-half of the cut from the bottom edge of the block.

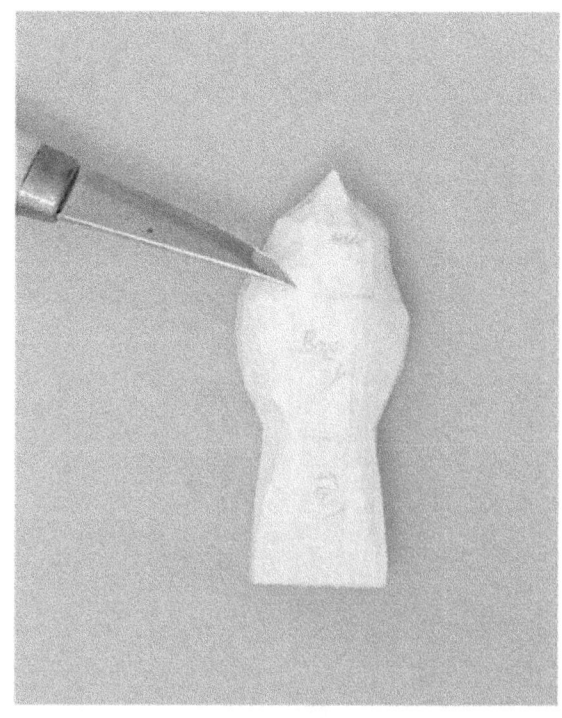

6. Shape the intersection between the head and the body. On the sides of the bird, use the push cut to whittle a gently sloping transition between the body and the head, using the upper horizontal line to start each cut.

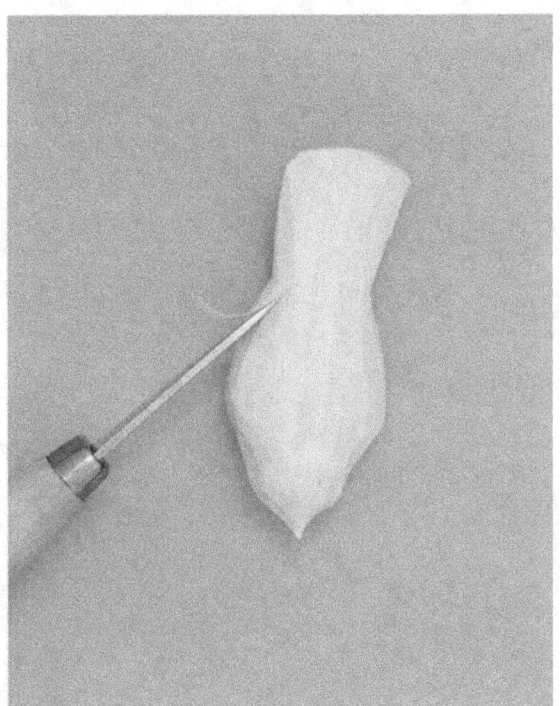

7. Round the hard corners. Use the push cut to round any hard corners and refine the bird's shape. Since this bird is meant to be held in the hand for comfort, it should feel smooth and even. If you are struggling to get a smooth surface with the knife, try sanding.

> **MIX IT UP TIP:** This simple project makes a great blank canvas to try out some detail techniques. Try adding eyes, wings, and some tail feathers.

Salad Servers

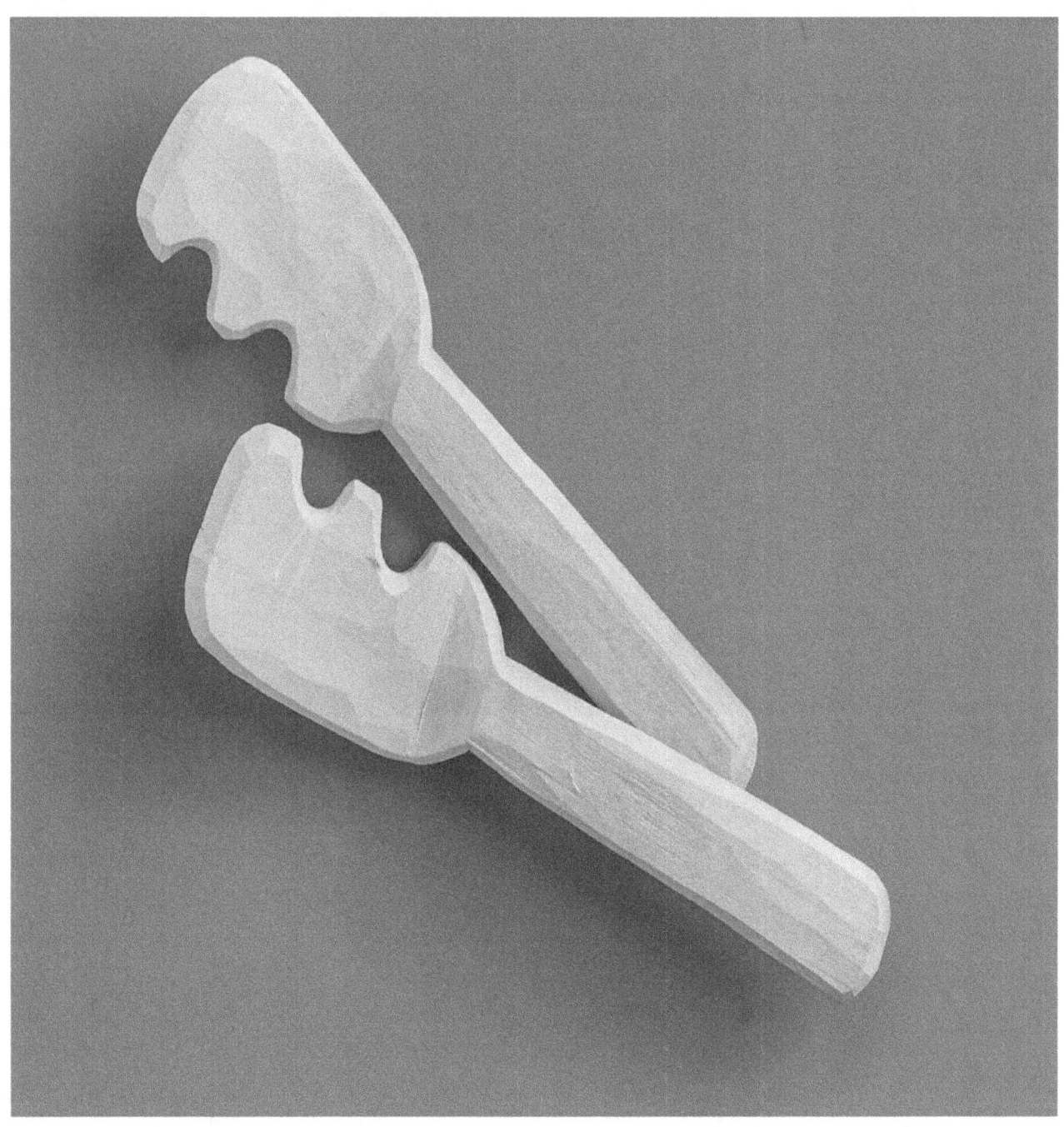

These salad servers are simple yet ergonomic. They require only a few measurements for reference and challenge you to make two mirrored items.

START-TO-FINISH TIME:
2 hours

WOOD DIMENSIONS:
2 similar blocks of basswood measuring 8 inches long, 2¼ inches wide, and 1 inch deep

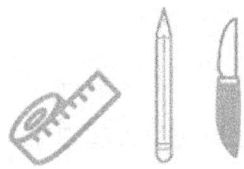

SUPPLIES:
Measuring tape, pencil, whittling knife

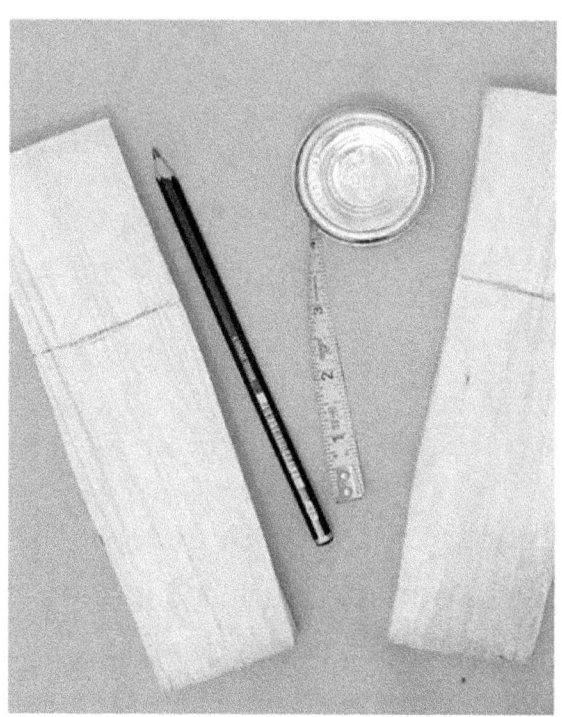

1. Mark the low point of each working end. The side profile of each server will slope down and then upward for ergonomics. Mark this low point around each block, 3 inches down from the top.

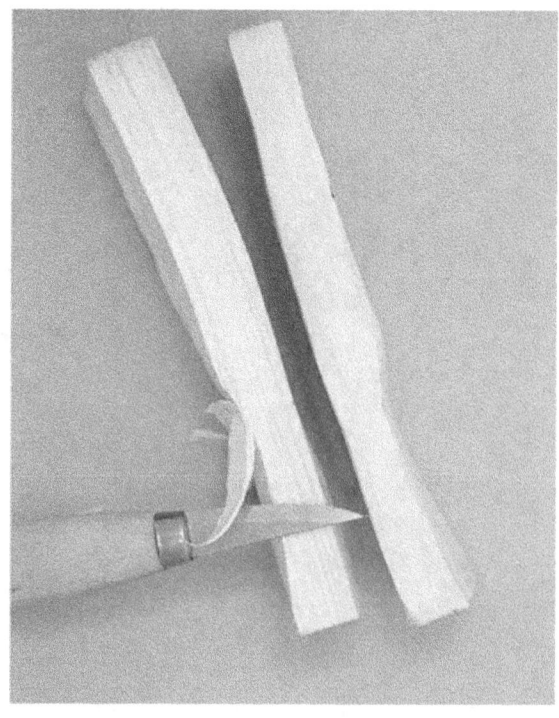

2. Whittle the low point. Using the pencil lines as a guide, whittle ¼ inch down, across each 3-inch face with the 2-sided push cut. Begin the cut 1 inch below the pencil line and meet it from the other side with a paring cut beginning at the top of the block.

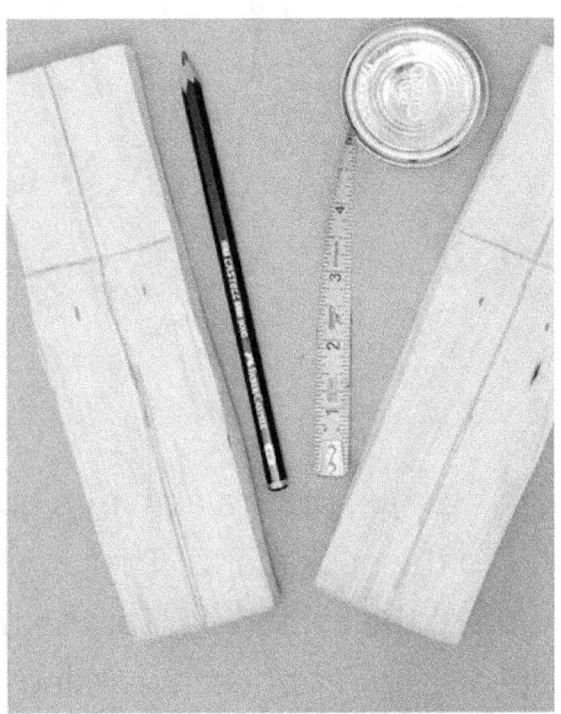

3. Mark the centerlines for the servers. Draw a centerline running vertically on the front of each server. Then, draw a horizontal line across each low point. At the beginning of the lower half of the push cut made in step 2, mark ½ inch on either side of the centerline for a 1-inch-wide neck.

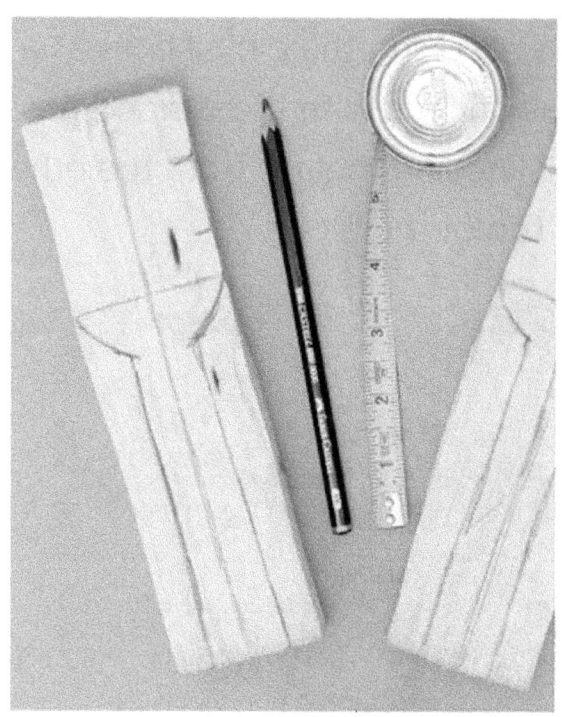

4. Draw the salad server shape. Draw a convex sloping line from the edge of each low point to the neck marks. Then, continue that line up the handle on either side of the centerline. For the tines, mark two ½-inch-deep lines on opposite edges of each working end, with 1 inch on either side of each mark.

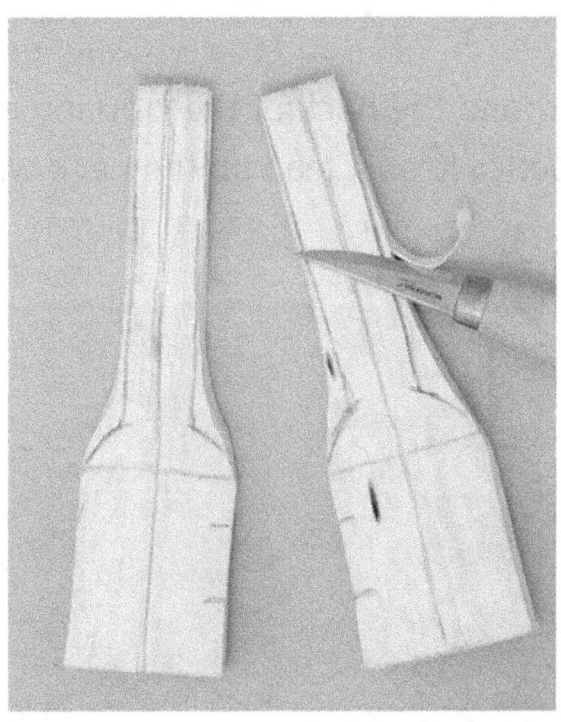

5. Shape the handle. Use the straight cut to carve the sides of the handle until you hit the pencil line toward the bottom. Then, use the push cut to clean up the rest of the handle. Repeat on the other server.

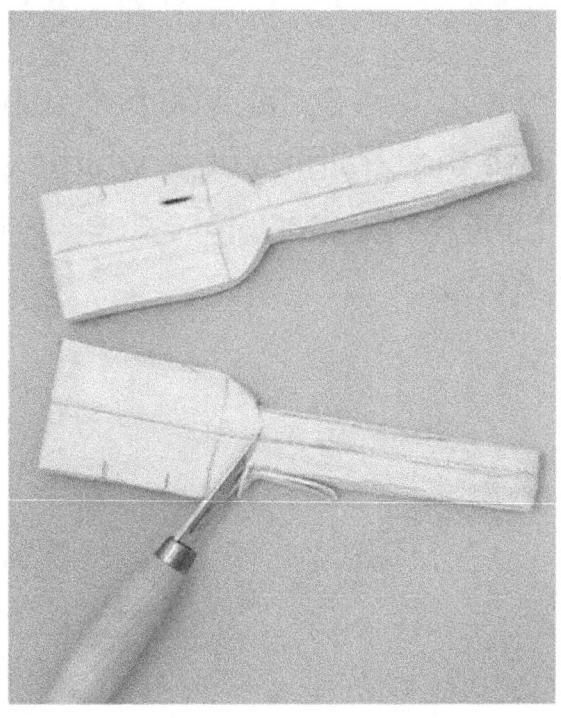

6. Whittle the intersection between the working end and the handle. Use the push cut to round the back of the working end of the server until you reach the pencil lines. Clean up the neck with a very controlled v-cut.

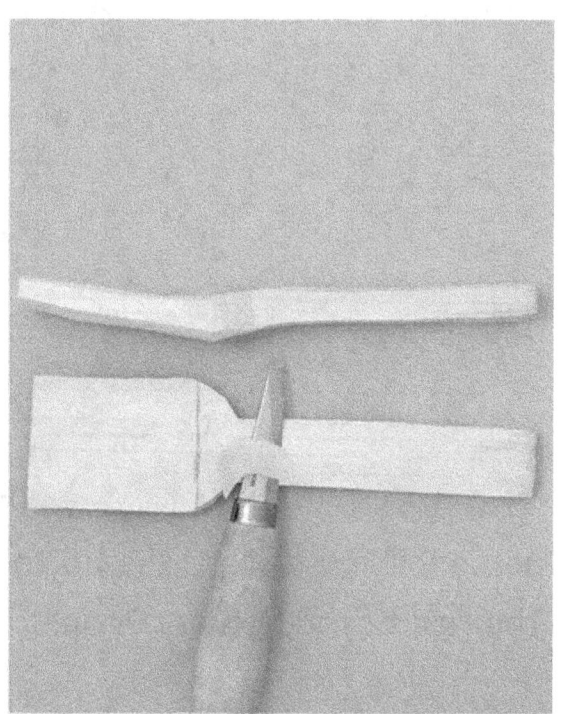

7. Thin the back of each server. So far, you have whittled each server's front face and sides. Use the straight cut to whittle away from both sides of the low point line on the back face of each server until the back face is parallel to the front.

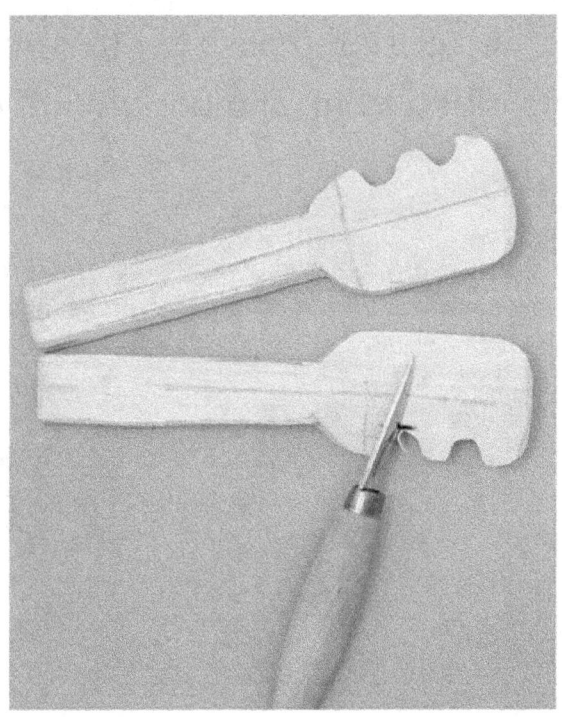

8. Carve the tines. Use the two-sided push cut to whittle each tine of the salad servers. Use each line drawn on the working end in step 4 for reference.

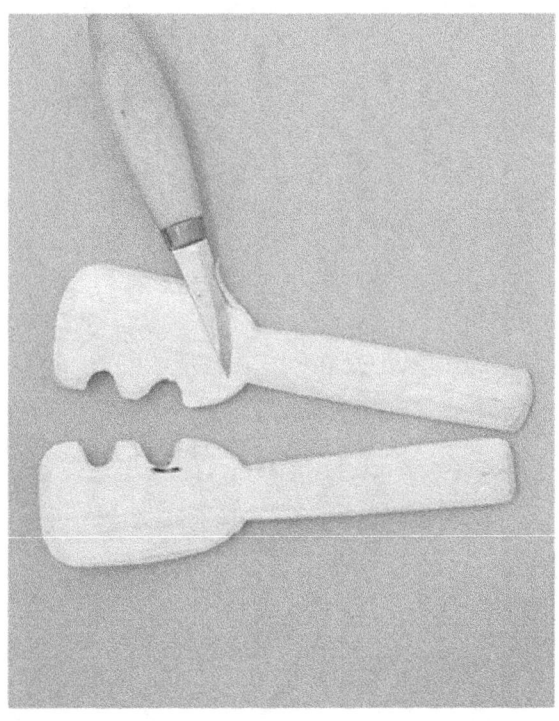

9. Round the hard corners. Use the push cut to carefully round the hard corners on the servers' sides, front, and back. Whittle away any residual pencil marks.

> **PERSONALIZE IT TIP:** This project guides you through drawing your own salad servers, but if you have a favorite set that you want to copy, try tracing them on the wood!

Perching Owl

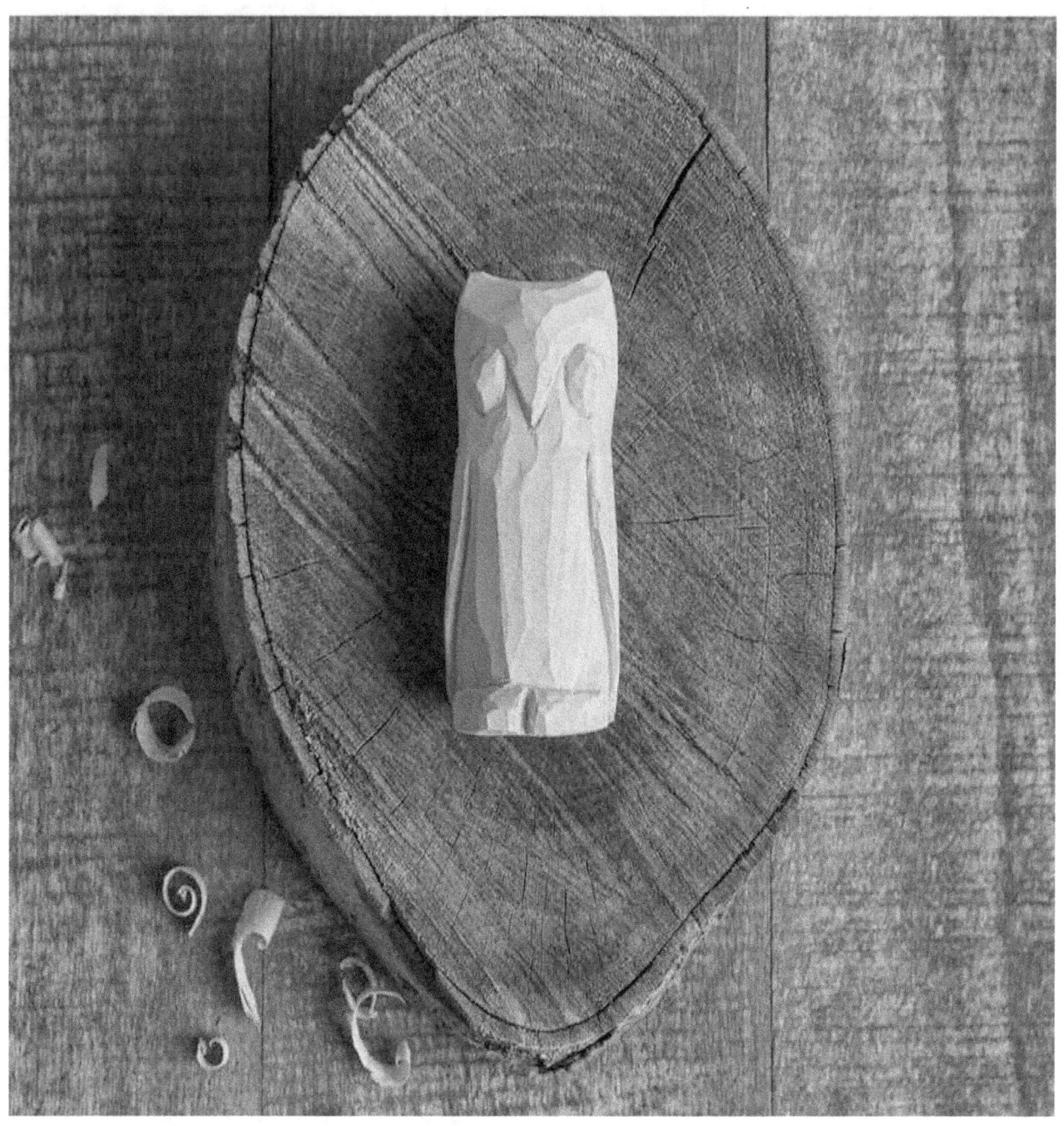

This owl carving is the first small whittling project without extra wood on the end to hold, so a carving glove on your nondominant hand is recommended for safety.

START-TO-FINISH TIME:
1 hour 45 minutes

WOOD DIMENSIONS:
A squared block of basswood measuring 3 inches long, 1½ inches wide, and 1½ inches deep

SUPPLIES:
Carving glove (recommended), whittling knife, measuring tape, pencil, detail gouge

1. Facet the vertical corners. Use the paring cut to carefully round the vertical corners of the basswood block. Continue until the block is an octagon (eight-sided) in the cross-section. These eight facets will give you easy reference points to make everything even.

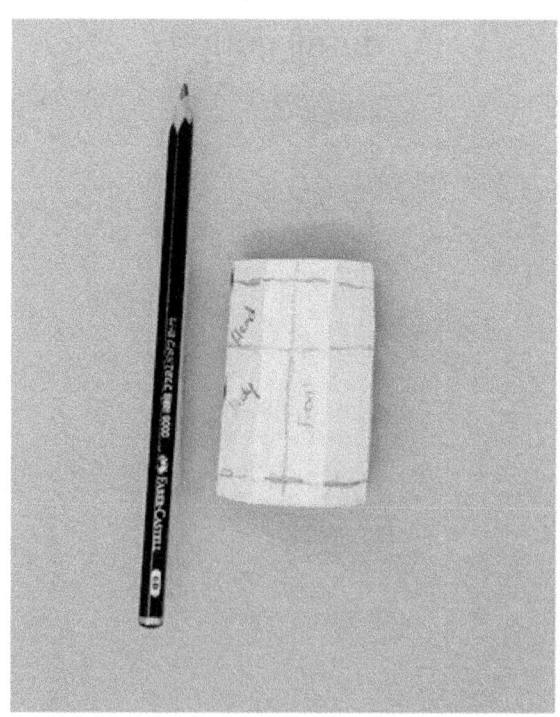

2. Divide the block into horizontal sections. Draw a line around the block 1 inch down from the top. Label the top section "head" and the bottom section "body." Draw a vertical centerline on the nicest facet and label it "front." Draw two lines around the block ¼ inch in from the bottom and top of the block.

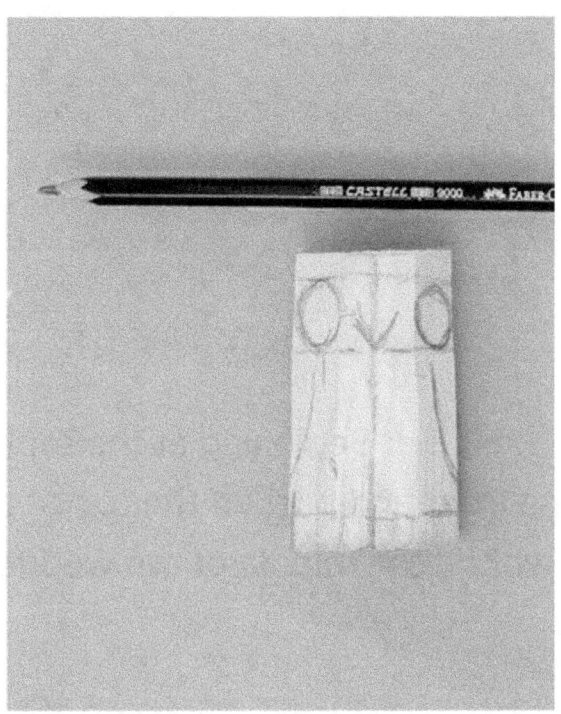

3. Draw the wings, feet, and face. For a beak, draw a "v" that meets at the bottom of the head section in the center. For the eyes, draw a circle on each of the left and right front facets. For the wings, draw a sloping line on either side, starting just below the center of each eye circle and ending at the base of the side facets.

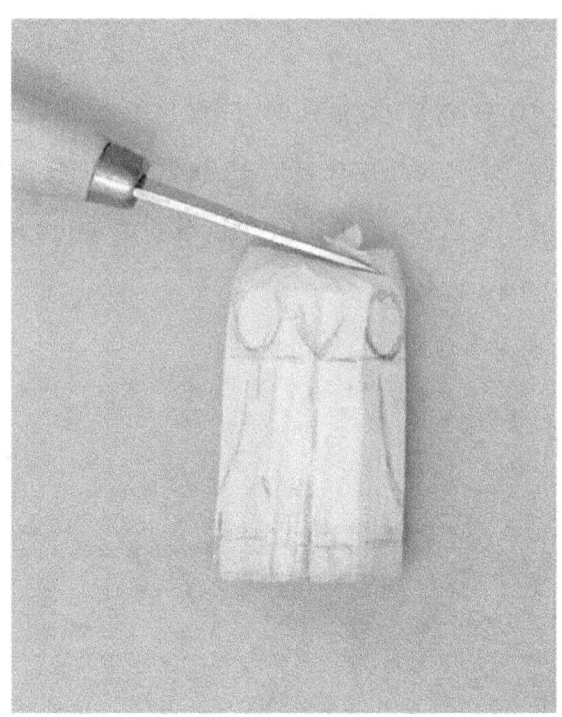

4. Round the top of the head. Beginning at the topmost line, use the push cut to flatten the front and back of the top of the head, shaping it into a wedge. Then, whittle the middle of the wedge, so the owl has two subtle ear tufts.

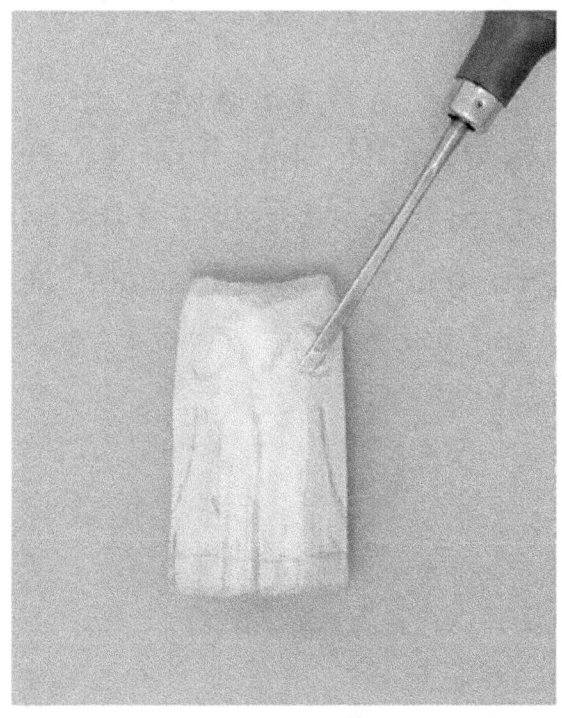

5. Whittle the face. Use the v-gouge to whittle along the beak lines and each eye circle. Then, use the skew chisel to round the hard corners of the beak and eyes. Use the skew chisel to shape the face toward the eyes and beak so that the features are raised above.

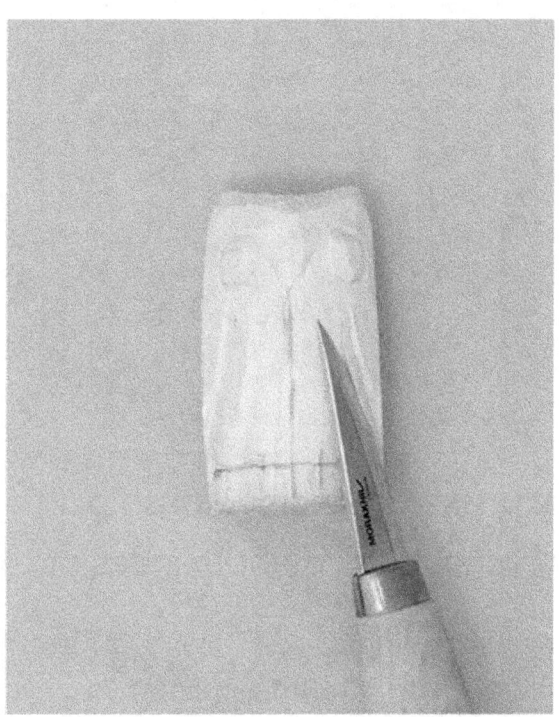

6. Shape the wings. Use a stop cut to whittle the wings. Make the 90-degree cuts on the drawn wing lines. Use your knife to round the body toward the wing lines.

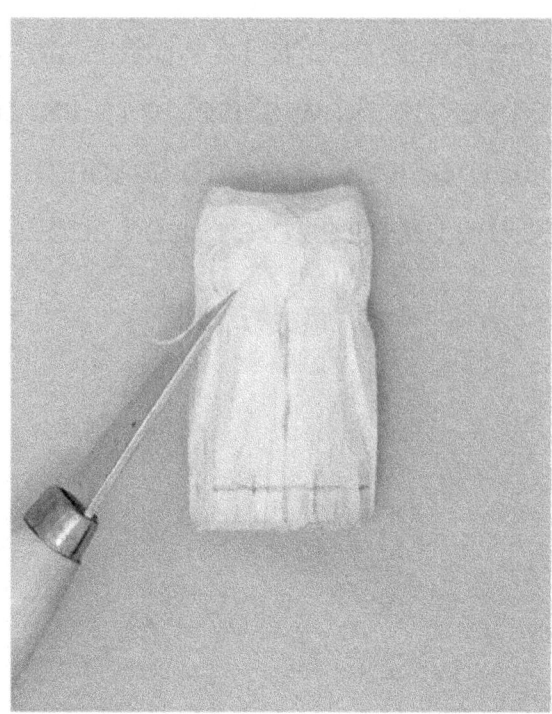

7. Carve the shoulders. Use the 2-sided push cut to carve a gentle divot between the head and shoulders on both sides of the block.

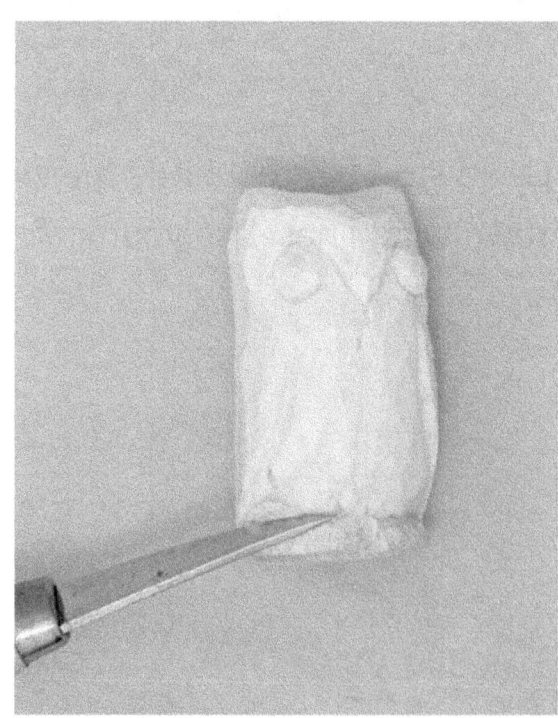

8. Carve the feet. Use a v-cut to whittle the horizontal intersection between the feet and body. Then, use the v-gouge to whittle the centerline in the foot section.

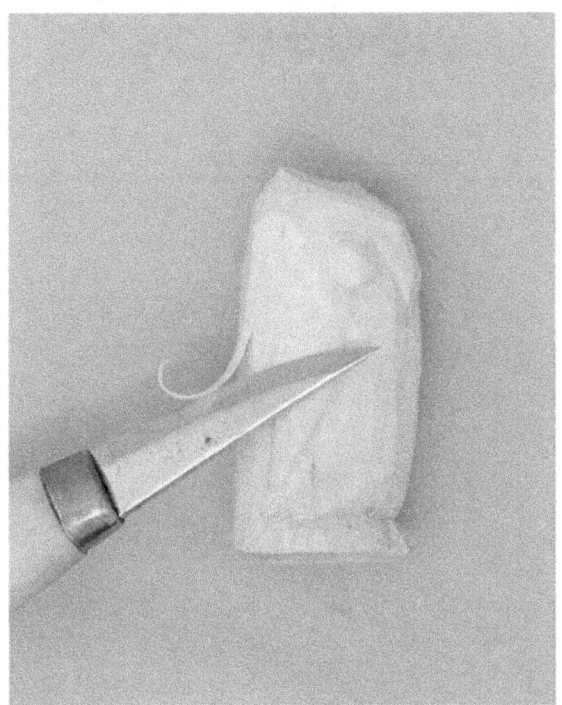

9. Round the back facets and clean up any hard edges. Use the push cut to clean up any remaining facets and hard edges. Then, carefully whittle away the pencil lines.

> **TECHNIQUE TIP:** Since this project doesn't have waste wood to hold onto, try using the paring cut any time you usually use the straight cut to maintain accuracy and control.

Lidded Box

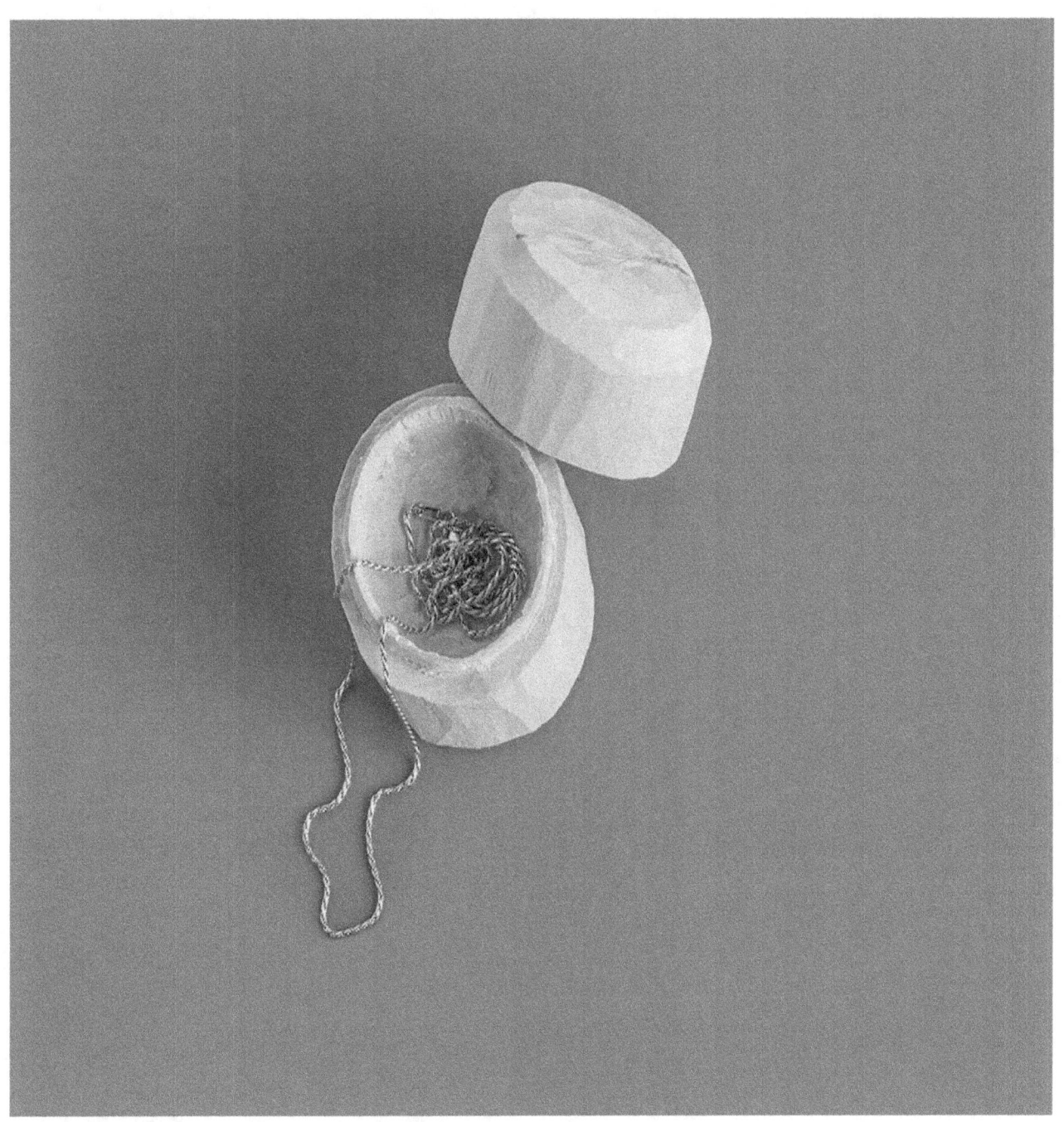

This small, rounded box has a removable lid. Everything is whittled out of a single piece of wood with the grain aligned vertically to give the edges strength.

START-TO-FINISH TIME:

2 hours

WOOD DIMENSIONS:

A block of basswood measuring 2½ inches tall, 2 inches wide, and 2 inches deep

SUPPLIES:

A 3-inch circle to trace, pencil, whittling knife, measuring tape, saw, detail gouges

1. Trace the circular template onto the wood. Center the template on the top of the wood block and trace it. Repeat this on the bottom of the block.

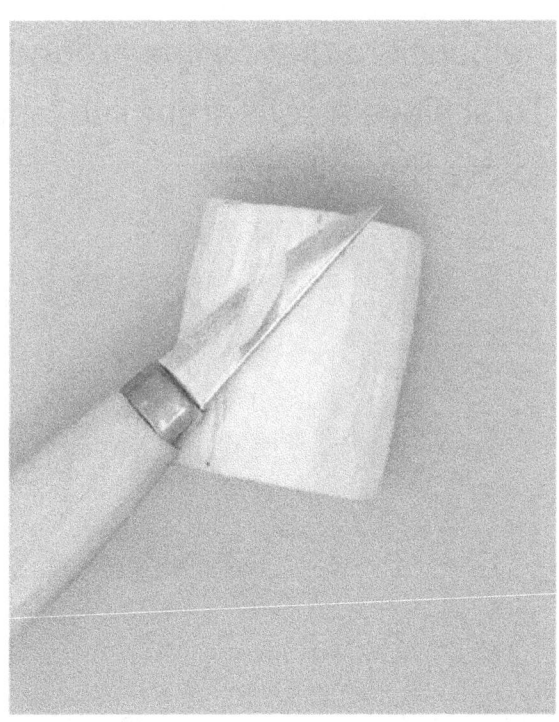

2. Round the side corners. Use the paring cut to whittle the vertical sides of the block, using the traced circles as a reference. The block should be cylindrical when finished.

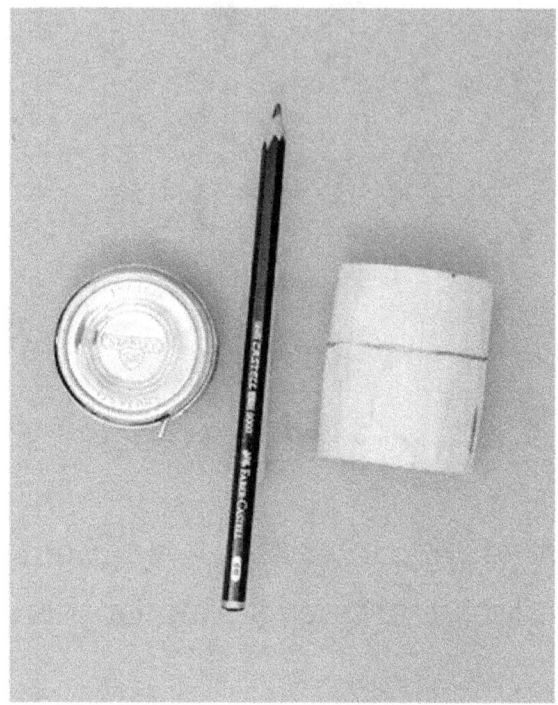

3. Mark the lid. Use the pencil to draw a line around the cylinder 1 inch below the top edge. To achieve a consistent line, anchor your hand on the top edge as you rotate the cylinder.

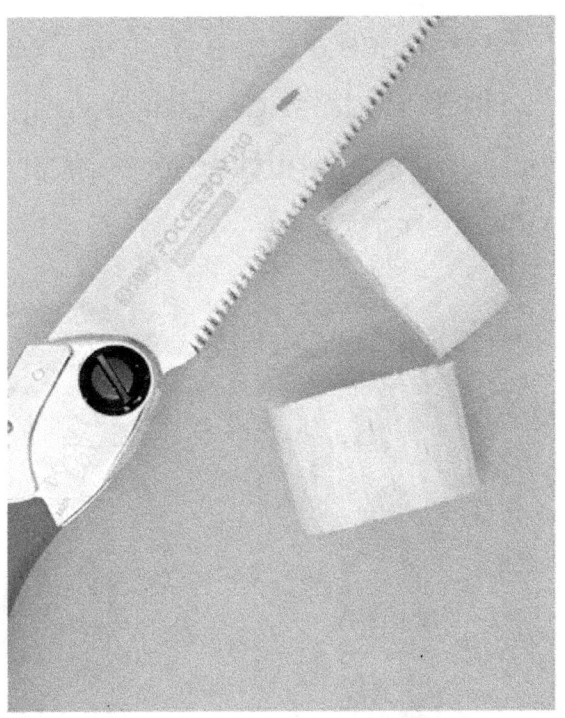

4. Saw apart the lid from the base. Anchor the cylinder on a work surface or in a vise and carefully saw along the line drawn in step 3. Take care to follow your lid line closely.

5. Hollow out the lid. First, trace a circle on the sawn side of the lid, keeping a consistent ¼-inch-wide edge. Using your curved detail gouge, hollow out the lid. Since you are whittling end grain, it is essential to make shallow cuts using a sharp tool.

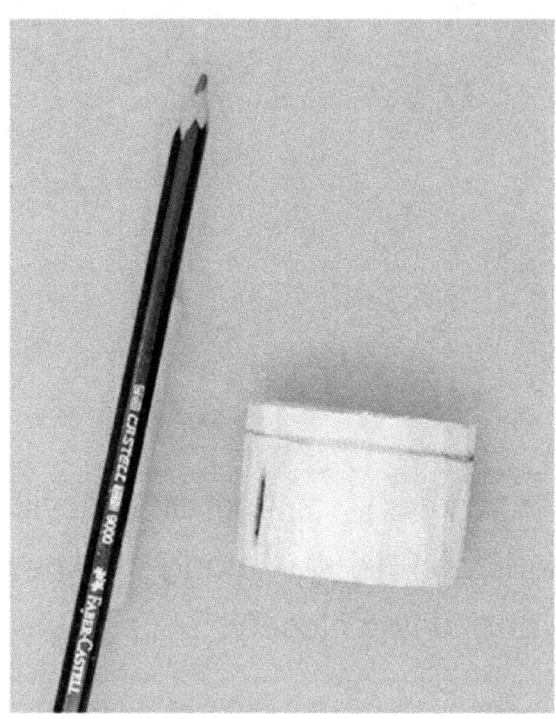

6. Mark the lip. Using your pencil, draw a line around the base of the box ¼ inch below the newly sawn top.

7. Whittle the lip. Use the stop cut to carefully whittle the lip of the base where the lid will rest. Use the line drawn in step 6 for the 90-degree cut, then whittle toward it from the top with the paring cut. Rotate the box after each cut for consistency. Continue until the lid fits on the base.

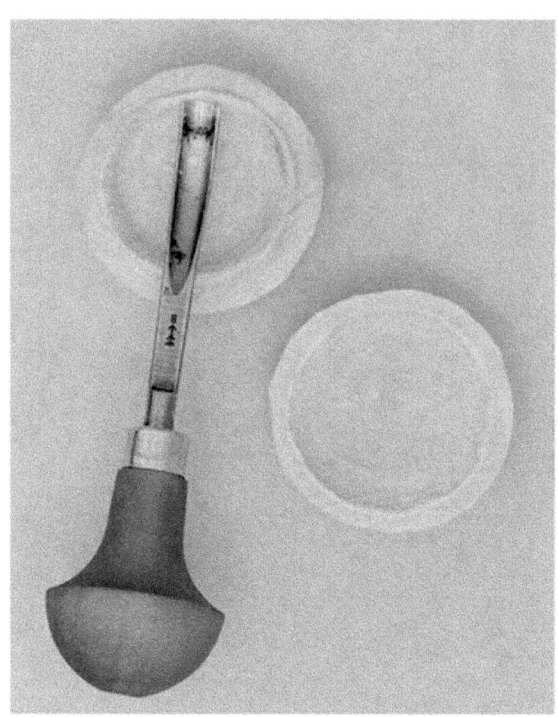

8. Hollow out the base. Once the lip has been whittled and the lid fits securely on top, use your curved gouge to hollow out the inside of the box, keeping the walls at least ¼ inch thick.

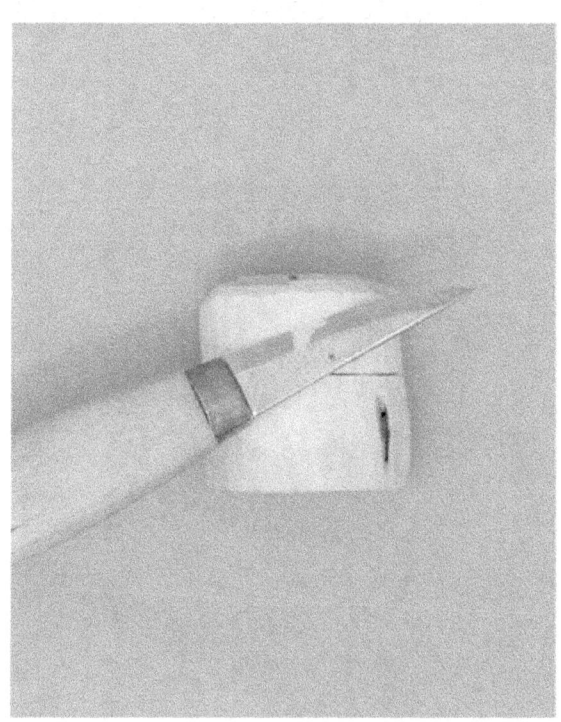

9. Round the hard corners. Use the push cut and paring cut to round the hard edges and clean up any inconsistencies between the base and the lid. It helps to put the two pieces back together for this step.

> **TECHNIQUE TIP:** If your lid fits only on the base in one orientation, try whittling a little hash mark with a detail gouge. This gives you a reference for where the lid fits best.

Whittled Whale

This finned friend makes a thoughtful gift. The facets carved in step 1 serve as reference points for several of the cuts so you can whittle the whale without a pattern.

START-TO-FINISH TIME:
1 hour 45 minutes

WOOD DIMENSIONS:
A basswood block measuring 5 inches long, 2 inches wide, and 1½ inches deep

SUPPLIES:
Whittling knife, measuring tape, pencil, detail gouge

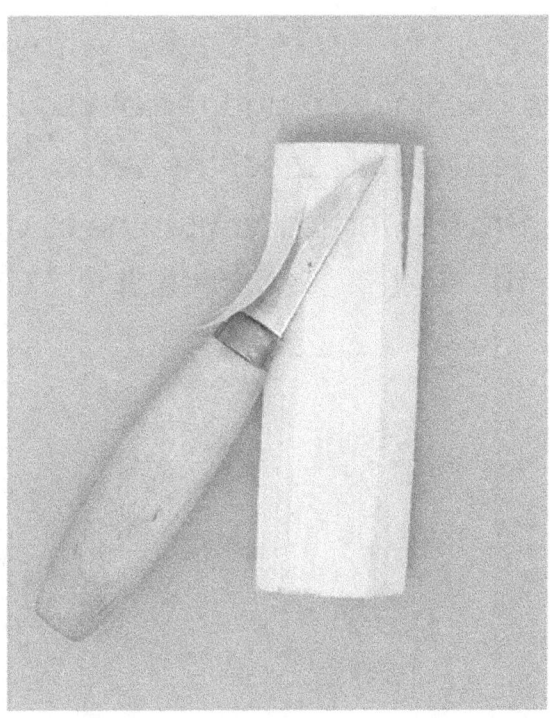

1. Facet the vertical corners. Use the straight cut to whittle the vertical corners until the block is a squat octagon (eight-sided) in cross-section. Make each corner facet the same size as the side facets, with the front and back facets slightly wider.

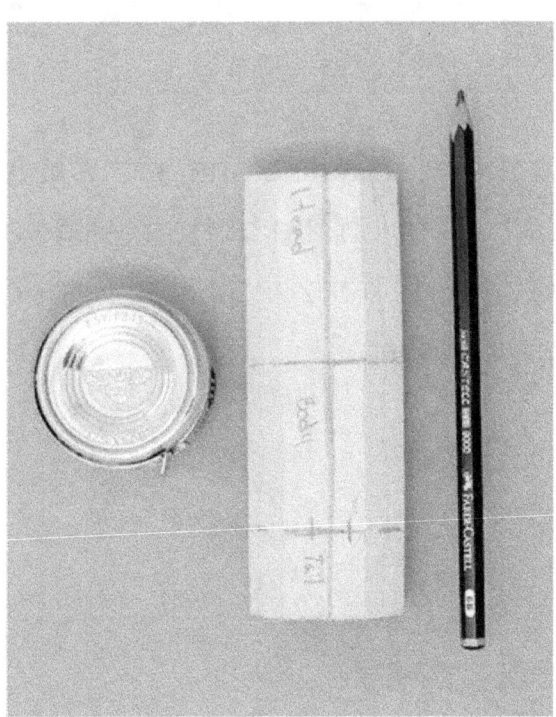

2. Divide the block into horizontal sections. With your pencil and measuring tape, draw two lines around the block, 1 inch up from the bottom and 2 inches above that. Label the sections "tail," "body," and "head," respectively. Draw a vertical centerline to divide the front face in half. Draw a mark on the bottom horizontal line, ¼ inch on either side of this centerline.

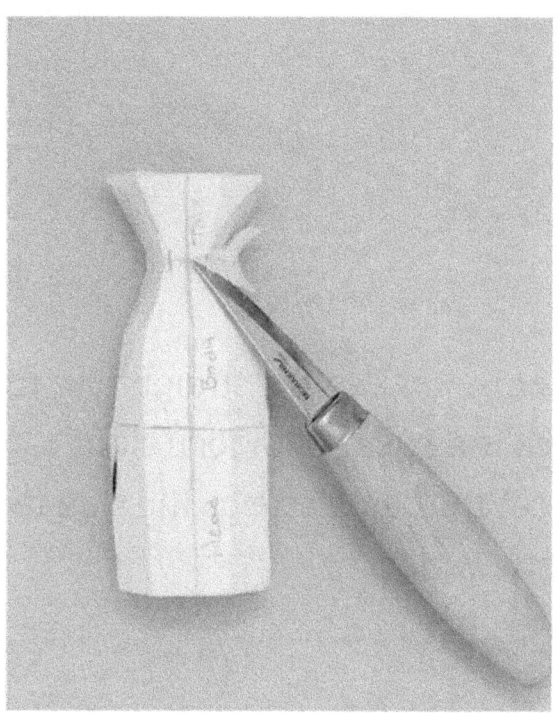

3. Shape the tail. Use the push cut to shape the side profile of the tail. Start the lower half of the cut on the bottom edge and begin the upper half of the cut at the topmost horizontal line. Continue until you reach the ¼-inch marks drawn in step 2.

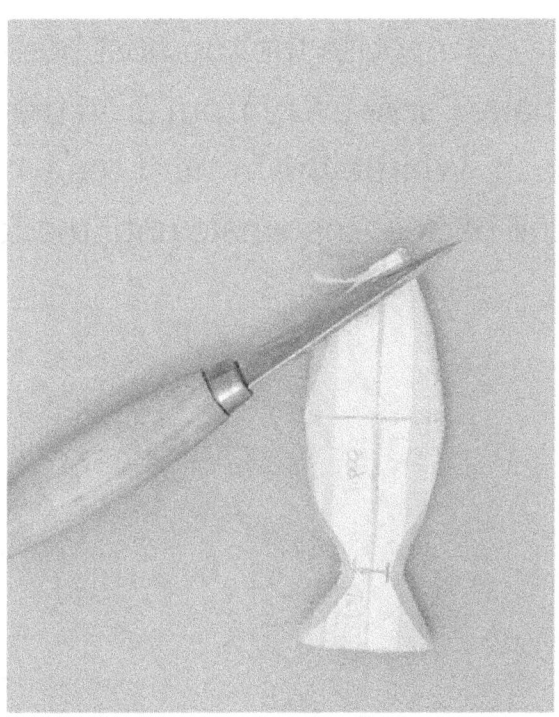

4. Shape the head. Use the push cut to round the top of the whale's head, beginning at the topmost line on the right side and gently sloping to the right edge of the front facet. Repeat for the bottom of the head and meet at the same point for an asymmetrically rounded head.

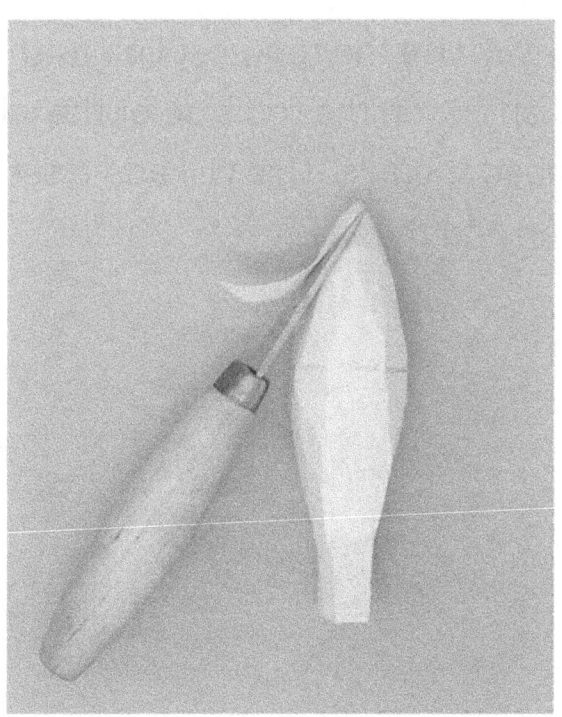

5. Thin the sides of the body. Use the topmost horizontal line as the wide point for the whale. Carve away from it on the front and back facets with the push cut. Whittle the front of the whale like a modified ball cut and wedge the back of the whale until the tail is ½ inch thick.

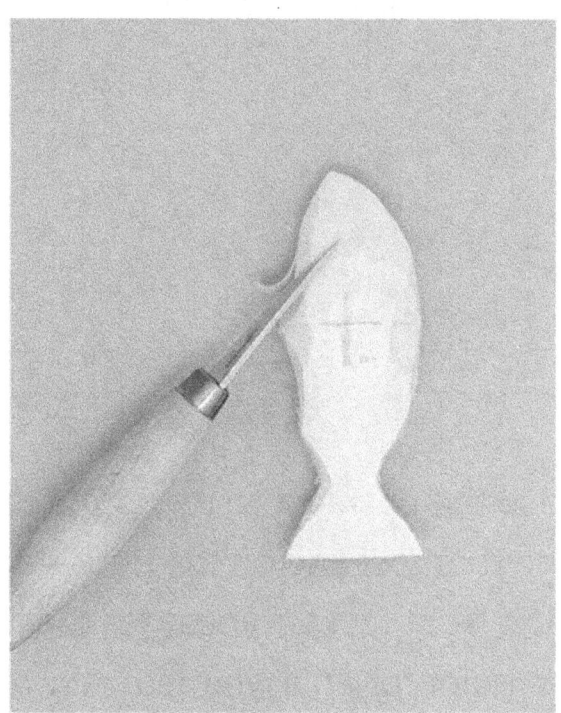

6. Whittle the dorsal fin. Use the topmost line as the high point for the dorsal fin. Use the push cut on the top side of the whale to whittle either side into a gently sloped triangle. This will add a second little bump between the dorsal fin and the tail.

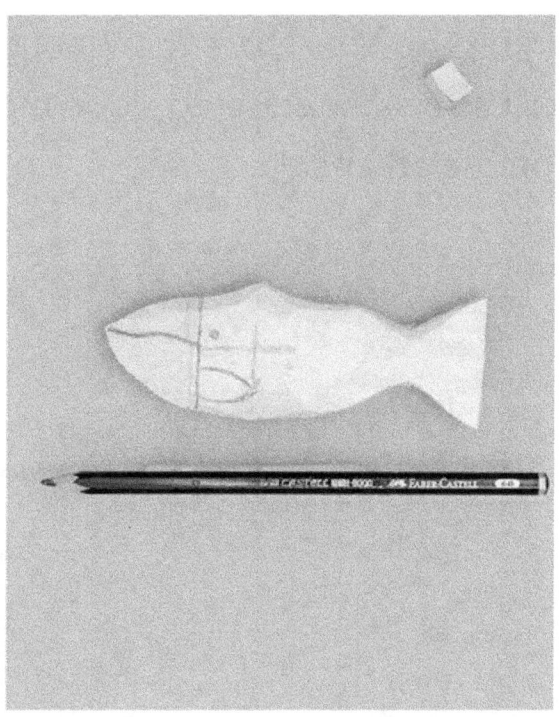

7. Draw the pectoral fin and face. Begin by measuring 1 inch down from the top of the block and drawing a line across. Draw a curved mouth from the nose to this line and an eye above it. Then, draw a fin ending at the left edge of the center facet. Repeat on the back side.

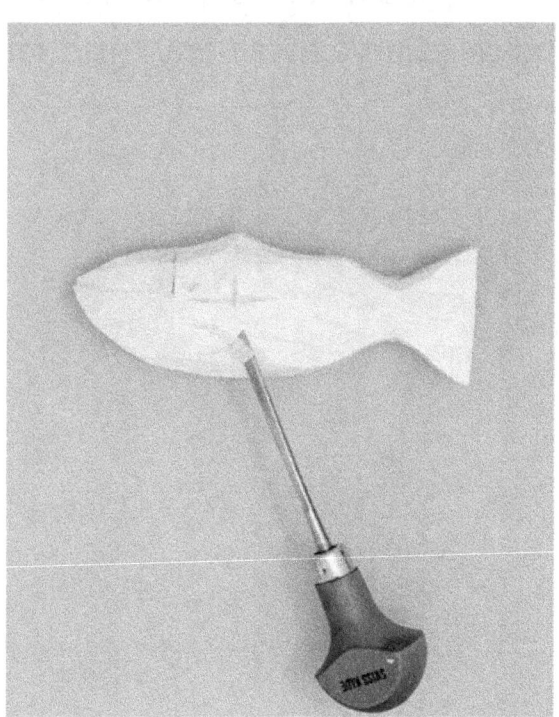

8. Whittle the pectoral fin and face. Use the v-gouge to whittle the lines drawn in step 7. Then, use a skew chisel to slope the body toward the pectoral fin. Repeat on the other side.

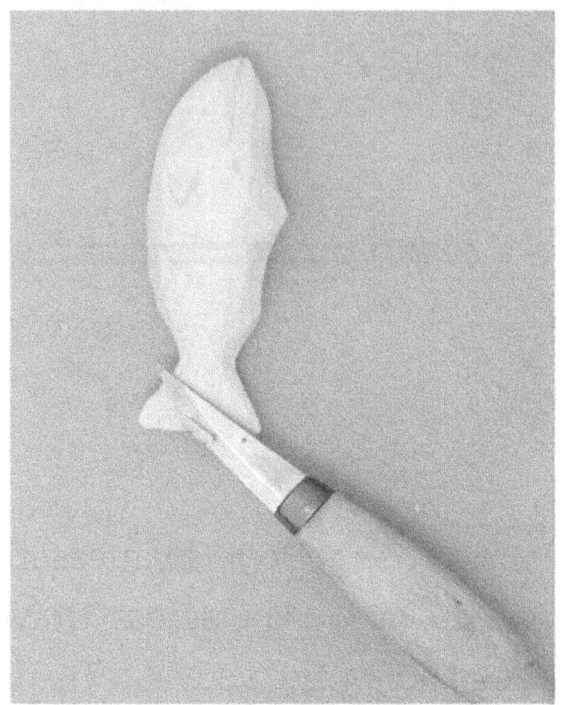

9. Round any hard edges. Use a careful push cut to round any hard edges of the body and tail. Carve away any residual facets and pencil marks.

> MIX IT UP TIP: There are many whale species with different body and tail shapes. Try altering these elements to make a specific type of whale.

FOUR

INTERMEDIATE AND INSPIRATIONAL PROJECTS

To achieve impressive intermediate projects, this chapter blends all the skills you have learned so far. Each of these projects is accompanied by a pattern and a few more steps to make them beginner-friendly. The patterns are designed to be printed, cut out, and traced directly onto the wood block. Some of the more intricate projects require you to make secondary cuts to the pattern to transfer details accurately. These projects challenge you to turn a two-dimensional image into a three-dimensional object by first whittling two-dimensional images and then rounding the project and adding details.

Whittled Spoon

Fox Figurine

- Toy Bear
- Garden Gnome
- Chess Pieces
- Wood Spirit

Whittled Spoon

Spoons are a fun and useful on-the-go project. The pattern will help you achieve an ergonomic spoon on your first try.

START-TO-FINISH TIME:
1 hour 30 minutes

WOOD DIMENSIONS:
A block of basswood measuring 7 inches long, 2 inches wide, and ¾ inch deep

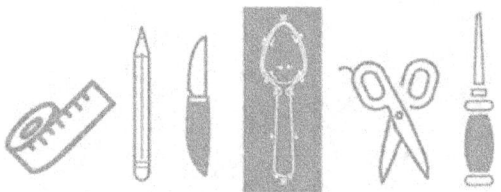

SUPPLIES:
Measuring tape, pencil, whittling knife, pattern, scissors, detail gouge

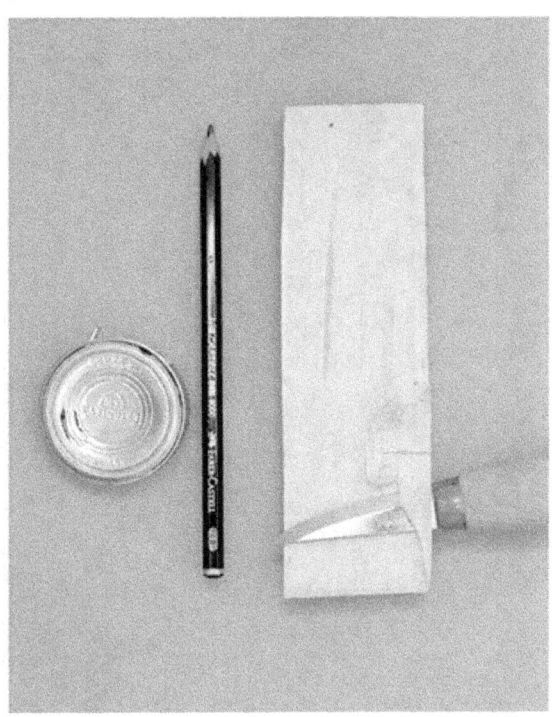

1. Whittle the low point of the working end. Draw a line around the block 2 inches down from the top. Starting 1 inch below the line on the front face, whittle toward the line with the push cut. Meet it with a paring cut starting at the top of the block. Continue until the low point is ½ inch thick.

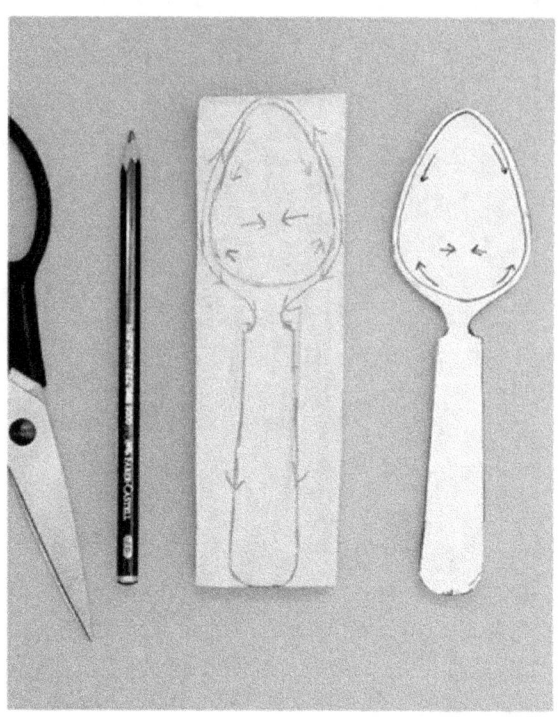

2. Trace the pattern. Cut out the pattern (you may want to copy it first and then cut it out) and line it up on the block's whittled face, so the bowl's widest point is at the low point. Trace the pattern and copy the directional arrows for carving.

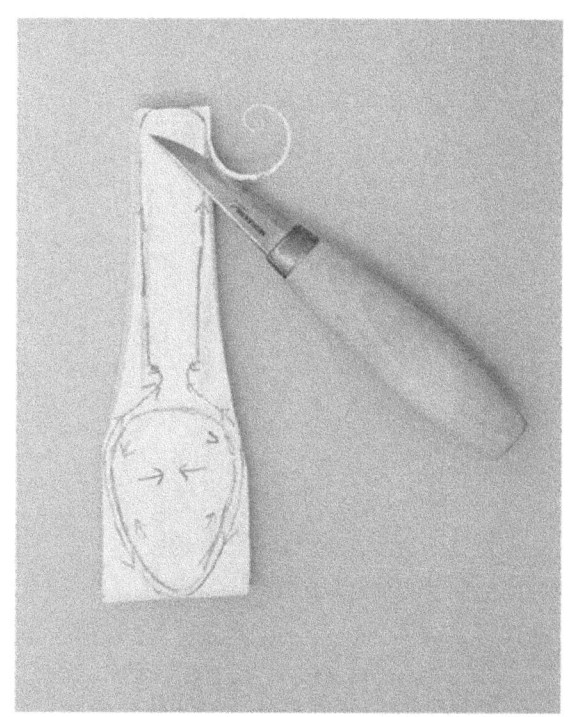

3. Thin the handle. Hold the spoon's bowl and use a straight cut to remove wood on either side of the handle. Continue until you reach the pencil line at any point on the handle.

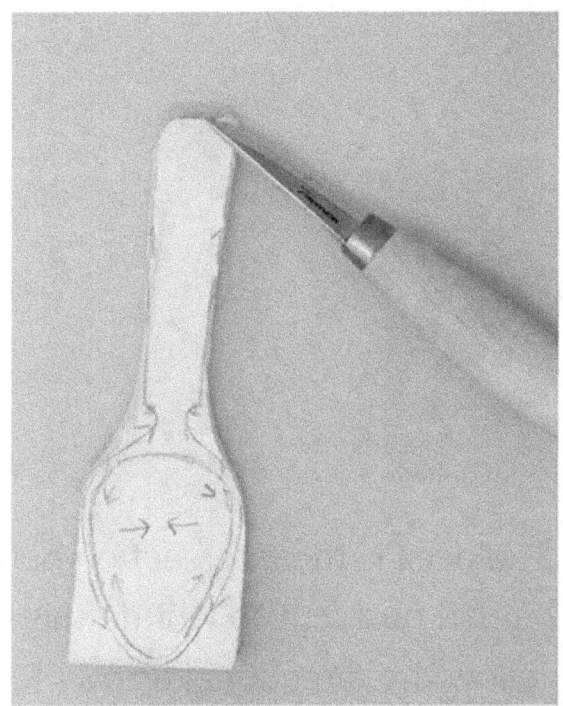

4. Shape the handle. Use the push cut to carefully whittle to the full pencil line on both sides of the handle. Round the end of the handle, but don't worry about the neck.

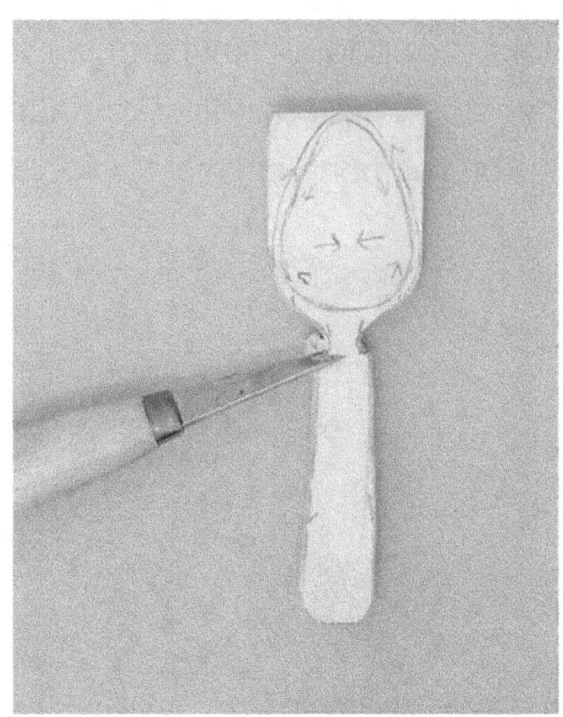

5. Whittle the neck. The neck is the intersection between the bowl and the handle. Use the 2-sided push cut to whittle this intersection on both sides, taking care to follow the directional arrows for carving. Carefully clean up the intersections with a controlled push cut.

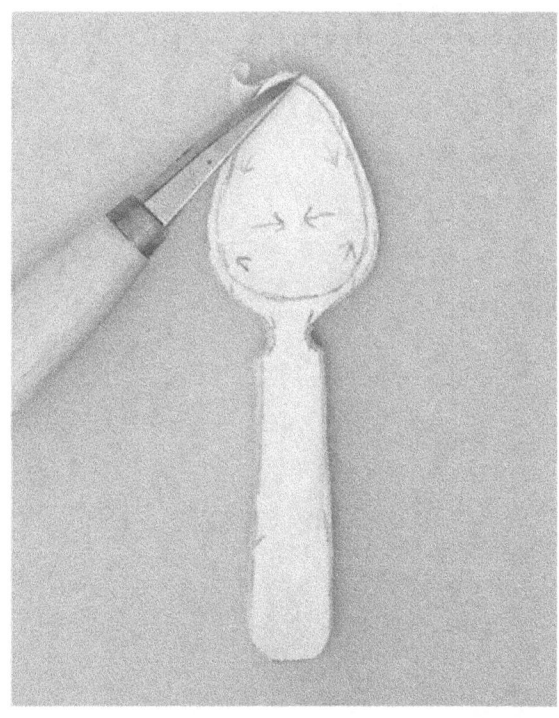

6. Shape the front of the bowl. Use the push cut to round the front of the spoon bowl until you reach the pencil lines.

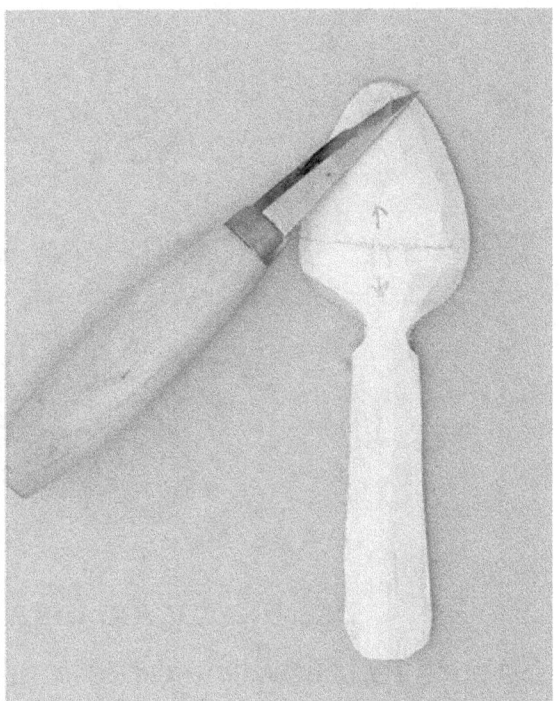

7. Carve the underside of the spoon. Carve the back of the spoon with the straight cut by carving away from the low point line on either side. Continue until the top and underside are parallel. Then, round any hard corners on the underside of the bowl.

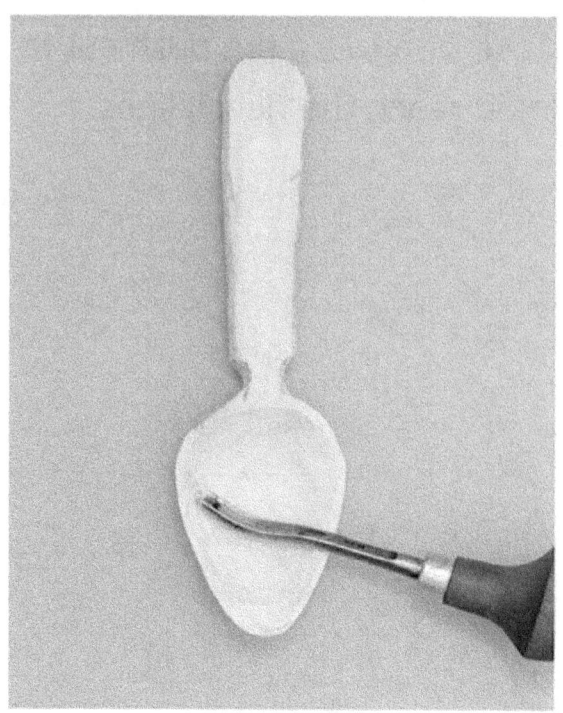

8. Hollow out the spoon bowl. Use the curved detail gouge to hollow out the spoon bowl. Be sure to follow the directional arrows on the pattern since they are the reverse of the outside of the spoon bowl. Continue until the walls of the bowl are even.

9. Round any hard corners. Use a push cut to round any hard corners. Thin the front of the spoon bowl until it is comfortable to use for eating. Round the handle, so it is comfortable to hold.

> **TECHNIQUE TIP:** As you hollow out the bowl, try pinching the bowl's walls in various places to test for an even thickness.

Fox Figurine

This project introduces a sawed stop cut to make the deep cuts that distinguish each leg more achievable.

START-TO-FINISH TIME:
1 hour

WOOD DIMENSIONS:
A block of basswood measuring 3 inches long, 2 inches wide, and 1 inch deep

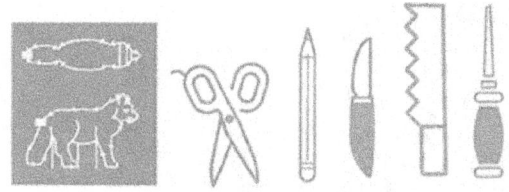

SUPPLIES:
Pattern, scissors, pencil, whittling knife, saw, detail gouge

1. Trace the top-view pattern. Cut out the top-view pattern (you may want to copy it first and then cut it out) and trace it lengthwise onto both 1-inch faces of the wood. Transfer the directional arrows for carving.

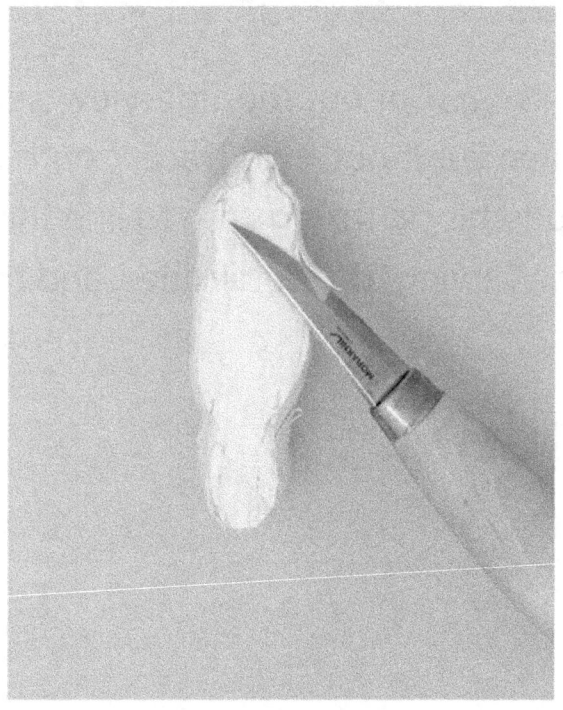

2. Shape the sides. Use the push cut to whittle to the pencil lines of the top-view pattern. Be sure to keep the 2-inch faces running parallel in order to maintain evenness in the final figure. Then, use the v-cut to shape the shoulder, face, and tail intersections.

3. Trace the side-view pattern. Cut out the side-view pattern (you may want to copy it first and then cut it out) and trace it onto both of the 2-inch-wide faces of the wood block, taking care to line them up. Transfer the directional arrows for carving, the detail lines, and the dotted saw lines.

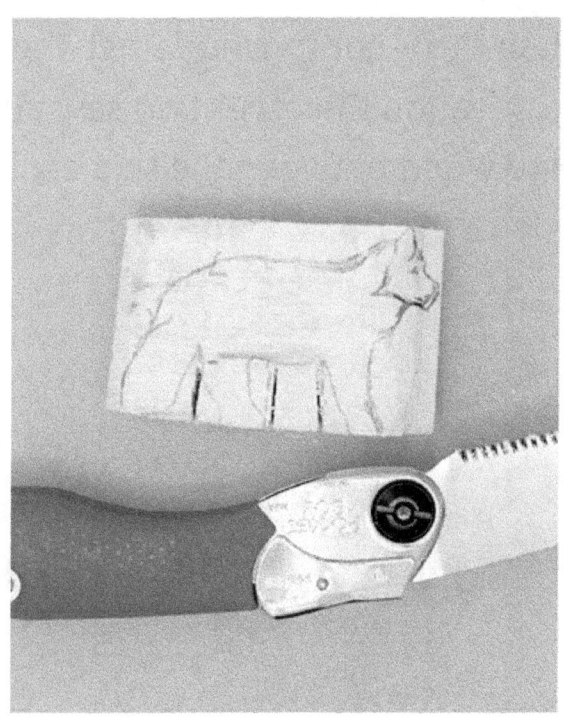

4. Saw the stop cuts. Saw along each of the dotted saw lines. Continue until just before the solid lines of the pattern. These saw cuts will make whittling the space between the legs easier.

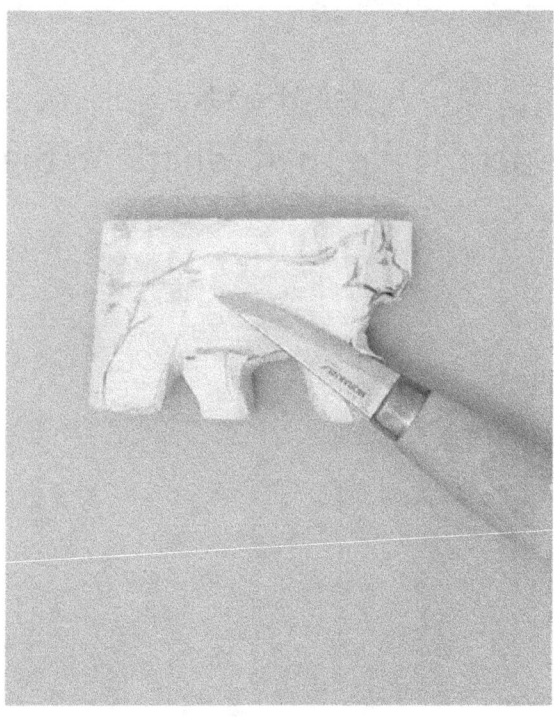

5. Whittle the legs. Use the v-cut to whittle between the legs toward the central saw cut. Repeat on the other two saw cuts. You may be able to chip away the waste wood between the two central stop cuts but be careful not to hit the legs.

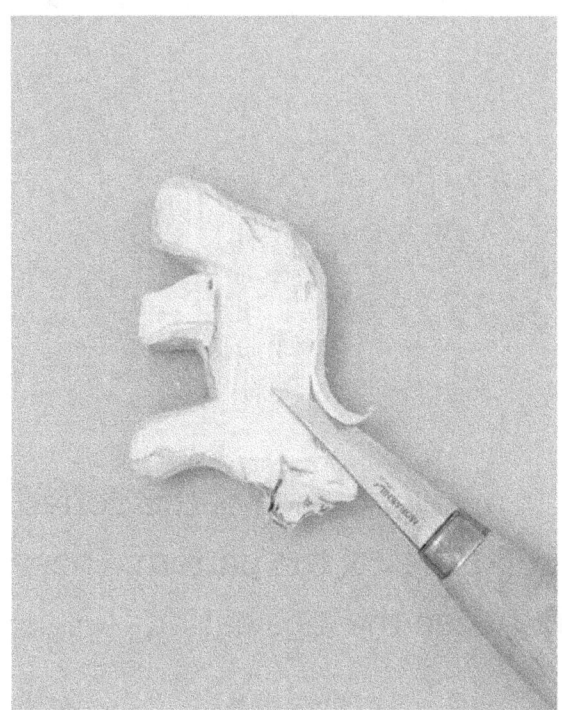

6. Shape the top of the body. Use the straight cut to whittle the fox's top until you reach a pencil line. Then, whittle to the rest of the line with a controlled push cut.

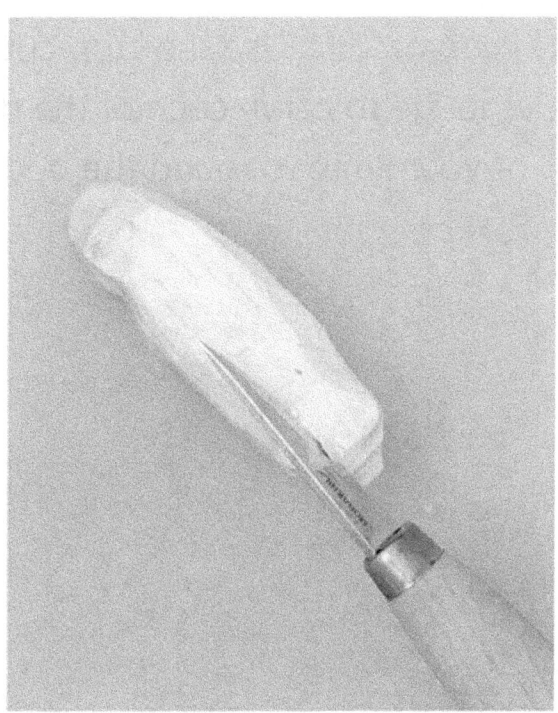

7. Carve the ears. Use the v-cut to whittle the front and back of the ears. Then, whittle another v-cut between the ears. Flatten the fronts of the ears with a controlled push cut.

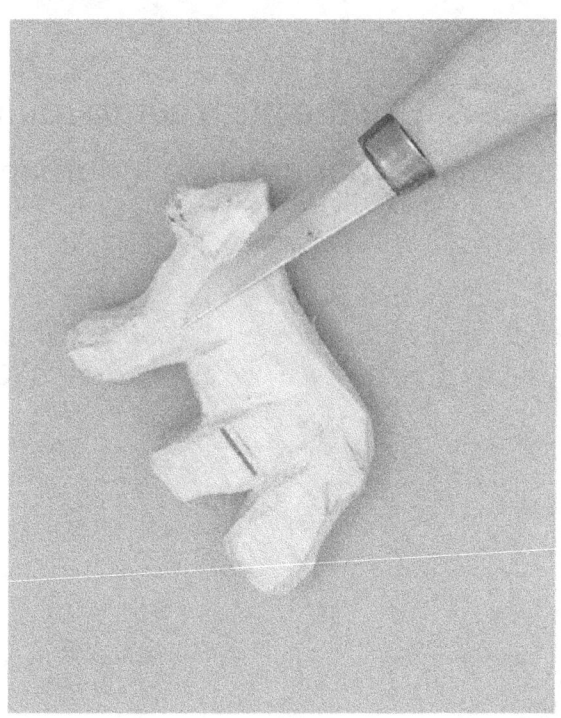

8. Whittle the face and leg details. Use the stop cut to whittle the brows. Then, use the v-gouge to carve each of the detail lines. Use the skew chisel or the tip of your knife to round the body toward the whittled lines.

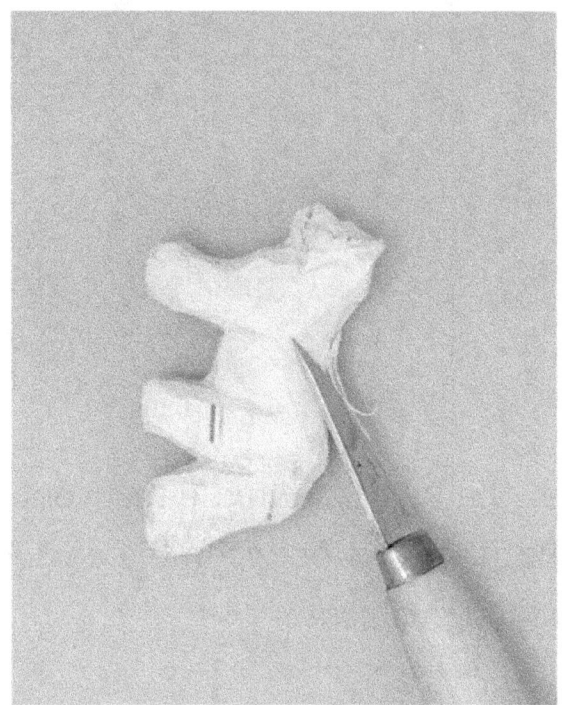

9. Round the hard corners. Use the push cut to round the tail and shape the body, legs, and neck. Use your creative judgment for the smaller details of the fox.

TECHNIQUE TIP: To make carving wide sections of wood easier, try whittling each corner to thin the wide face and then flatten the face by carving the entire face flat.

Toy Bear

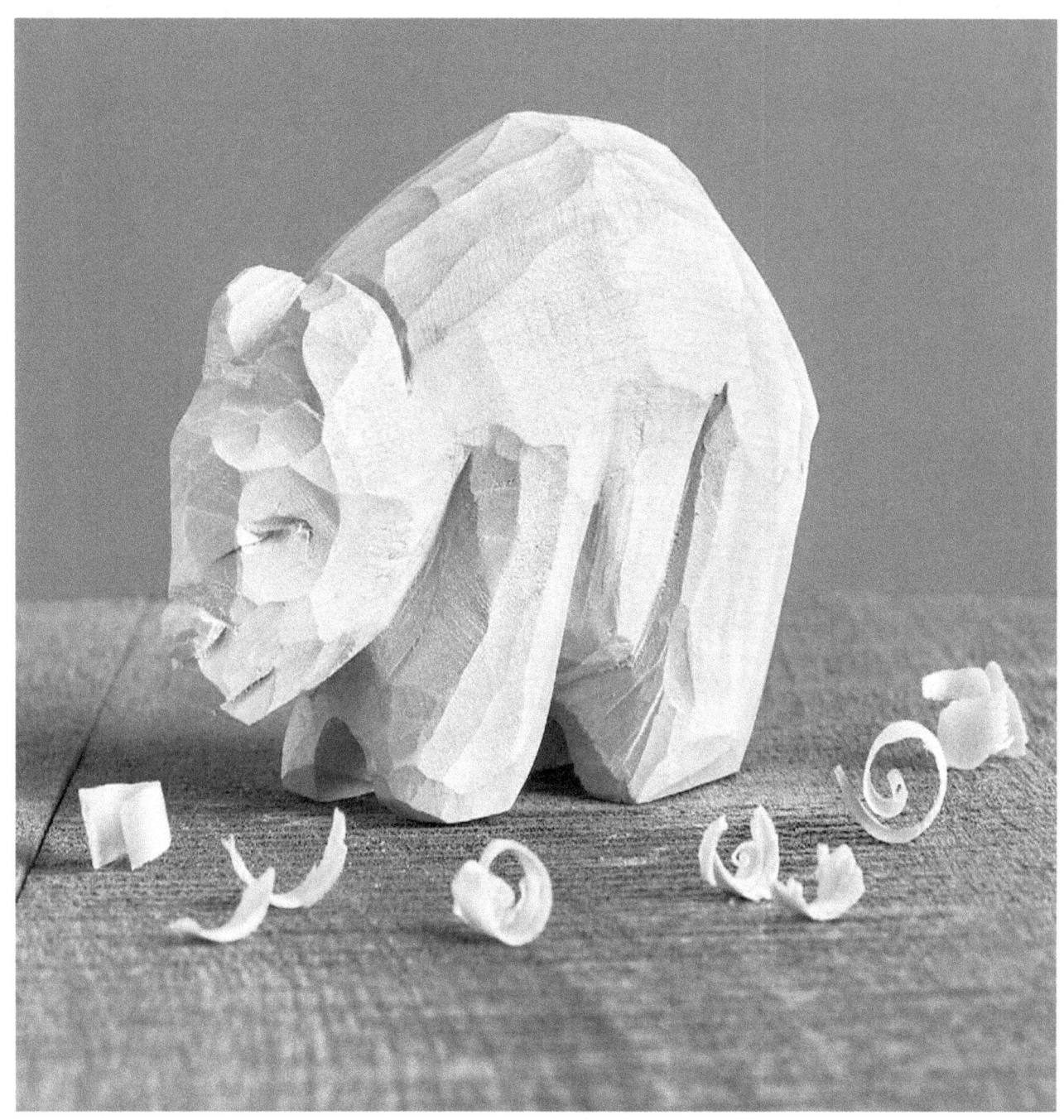

A whittled bear is one of the larger carved figures in this book. It makes a thoughtful gift for nature-loving kids and adults alike.

START-TO-FINISH TIME:
2 hours

WOOD DIMENSIONS:
A block of basswood measuring 4 inches long, 2½ inches wide, and 1½ inches deep

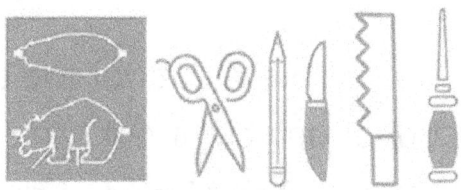

SUPPLIES:
Pattern, scissors, pencil, whittling knife, saw, detail gouge

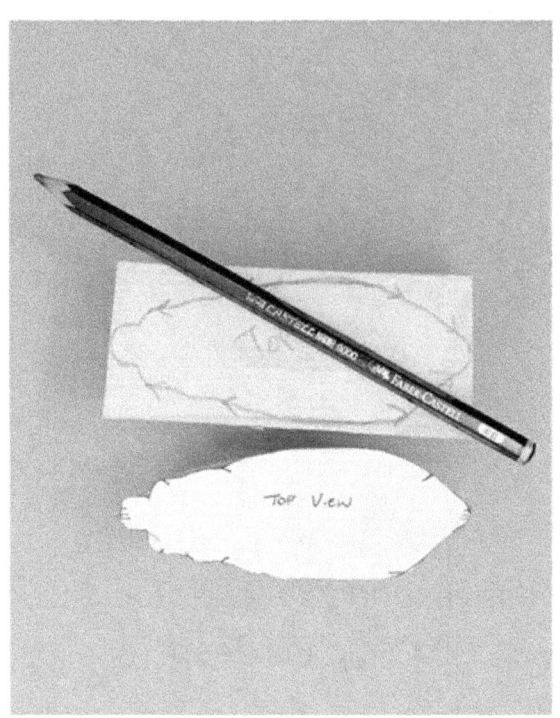

1. Transfer the top view of the bear. Cut out the top-view pattern (you may want to copy it first and then cut it out) and transfer the pattern onto both of the 1½-inch-wide faces. Copy the directional arrows for carving.

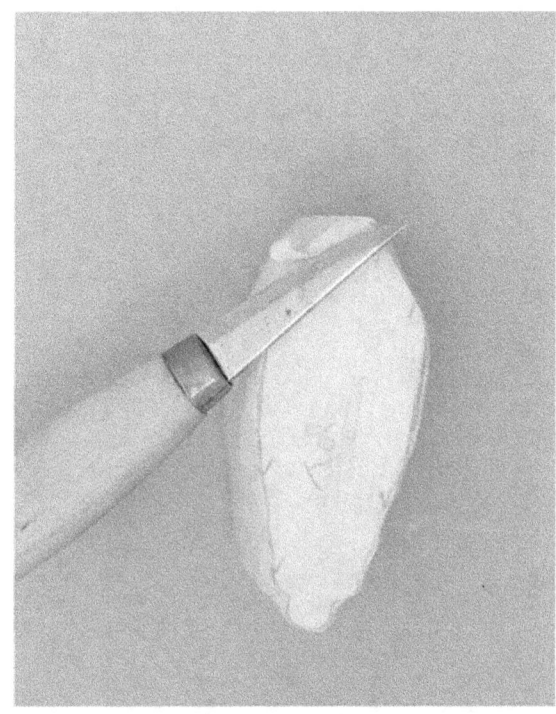

2. Whittle the sides. First, use the straight cut to remove wood from the sides of the bear. Then, use the push cut to shape the sides to the pencil lines. Be sure to carve the side walls flat and even enough to transfer the side-view pattern.

3. Transfer the side-view pattern. Cut out the side-view pattern (you may want to copy if first and then cut it out) and trace it onto both of the 2½-inch-wide faces of the wood block, taking care to line up the pattern on either side. Transfer the dotted saw lines, detail lines, and directional arrows for carving.

4. Saw the stop cuts. Since the space between the legs and the neck requires deep cuts, a sawed stop cut is more effective than a 90-degree knife cut. Saw along the dotted lines in the pattern, ending just before the solid lines.

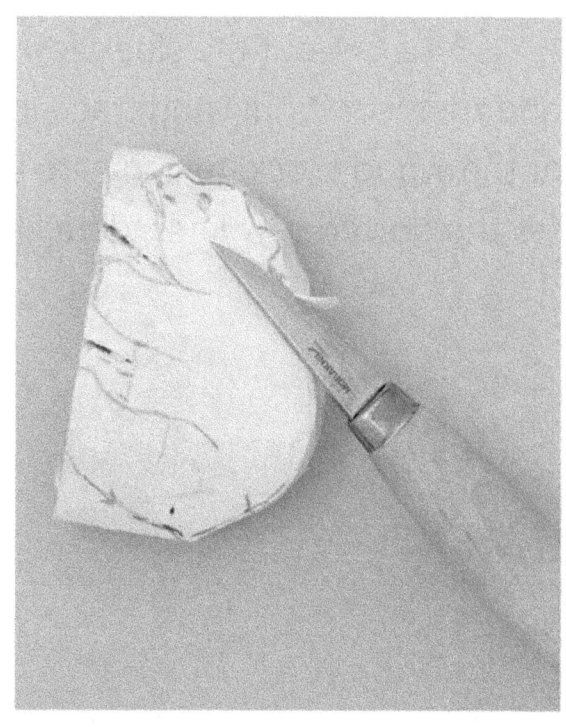

5. Whittle the back of the bear. Use the push cut to round the bear's back. Continue until you reach the pencil lines on the back half of the bear and until you reach the top of the ears on the front half of the bear.

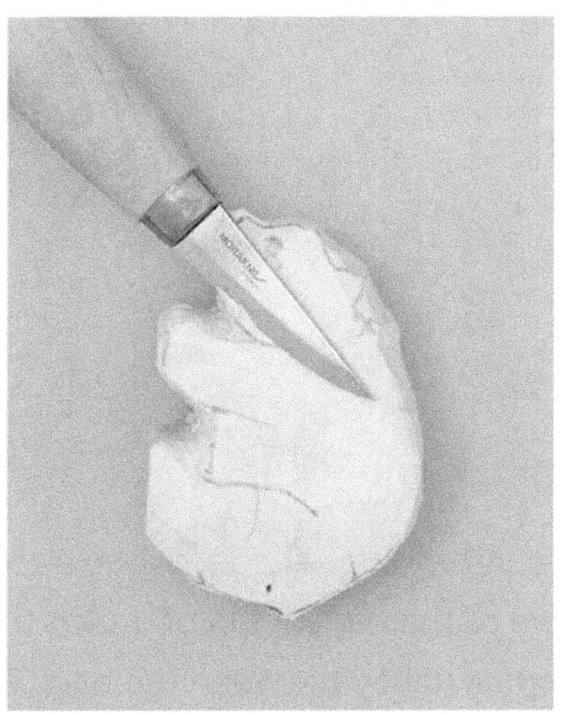

6. Carve the profile of the legs, neck, and head. Use the v-cut to whittle the space between the front and back legs. Use the push cut to shape the bear's snout. Use the paring cut to carve the bottom of the neck.

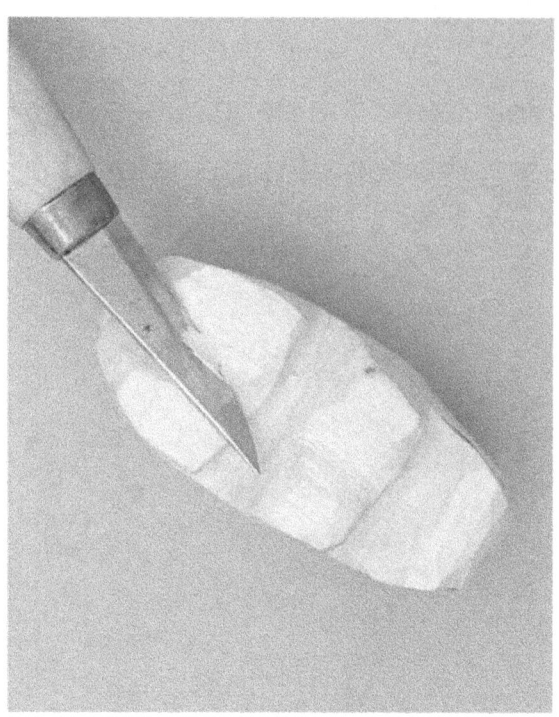

7. Shape the ears and in between the feet. Use a stop cut to whittle the front and back corners of the ears until you reach the pencil lines. Then, use a push cut to shape a valley between the ears. Repeat on the legs.

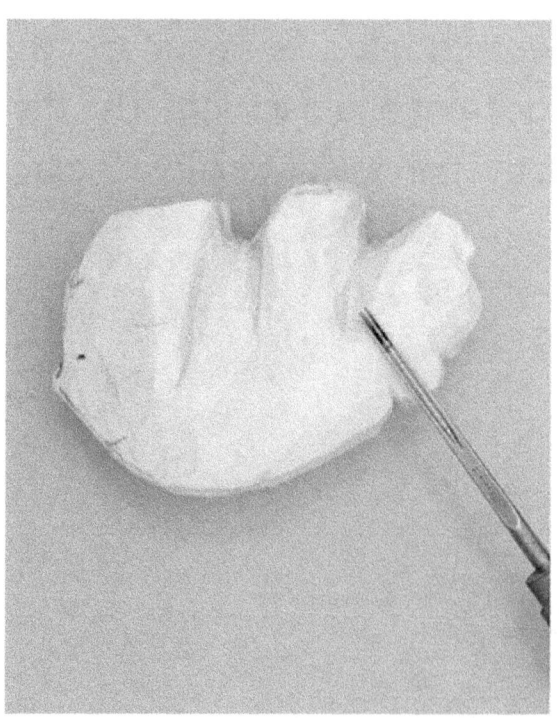

8. Whittle the details. Use the v-gouge to whittle the detail lines of the bear, including the eyes, snout, and haunches. Then, use the skew chisel to round the hard edges of the details and slope the body toward them. Use the curved detail gouge to clean up the valleys between the feet and ears.

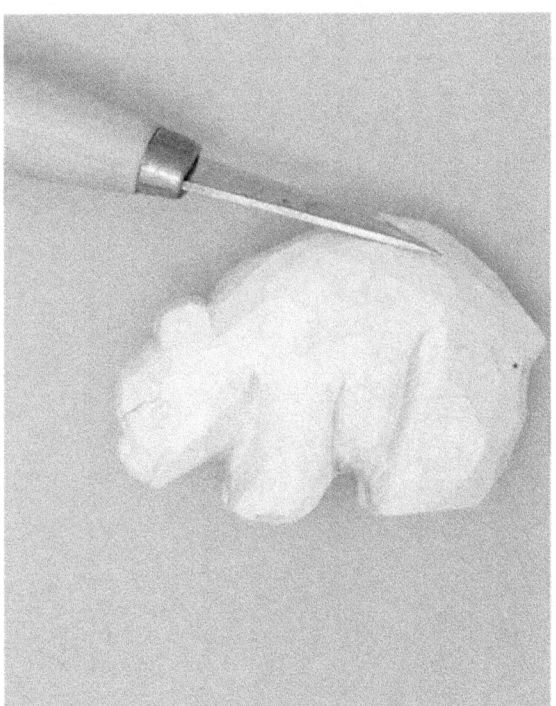

9. Round the hard corners. Use the push cut to round all remaining hard edges carefully. Whittle away any leftover pencil lines.

> **MIX IT UP TIP:** Try staining or painting your bear to make it a particular species. Try making the body a darker color than the snout.

Garden Gnome

Whether you need a mischievous gift for a friend's houseplant or a decoration for your garden, this simple gnome is guaranteed to delight.

START-TO-FINISH TIME:
1 hour 30 minutes

WOOD DIMENSIONS:
A block of basswood measuring 4 inches long, 2 inches wide, and 1¼ inches deep

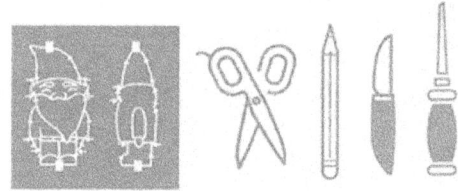

SUPPLIES:
Pattern, scissors, pencil, whittling knife, detail gouge

1. Trace the side-view pattern. Cut out the side-view pattern (you may want to copy it first and then cut it out) and trace the pattern onto the 1¼-inch-wide faces of the block. Make sure you mirror the pattern, so the toes face front on either side.

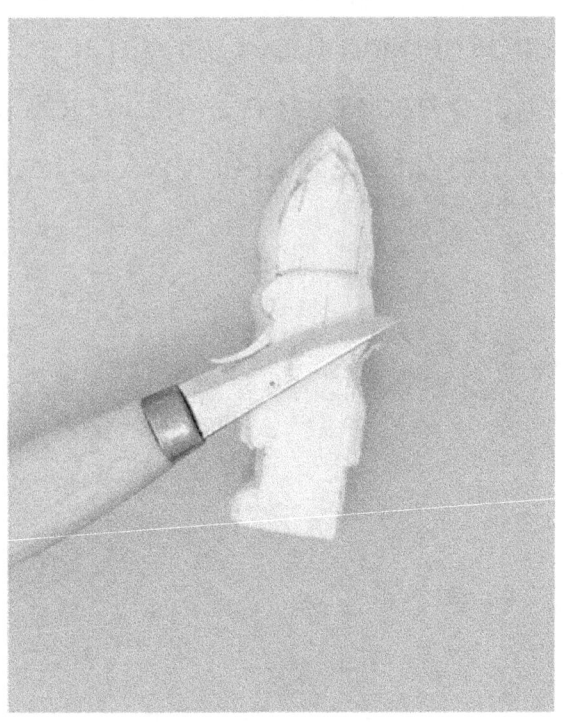

2. Whittle the side view. Use the push cut to taper the hat and shape the body. Then, use the v-cut to whittle the nose. Use the stop cut to whittle the bottom of the shirt and the top of the boots.

3. Trace the front-view pattern. Cut out the front-view pattern (you may want to copy it first and then cut it out) and trace the outer lines of the pattern onto the front and back of the 2-inch-wide face of the basswood block. Copy the directional arrows for carving.

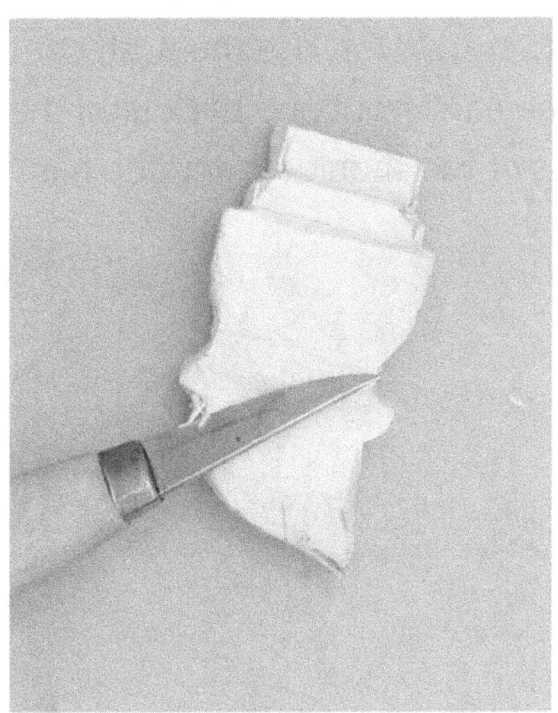

4. Whittle the front view. Use the straight cut to remove the excess wood from the sides, particularly around the hat. Then, use the push cut to shape the rest of the front-view profile. Use the v-cut to whittle the ears.

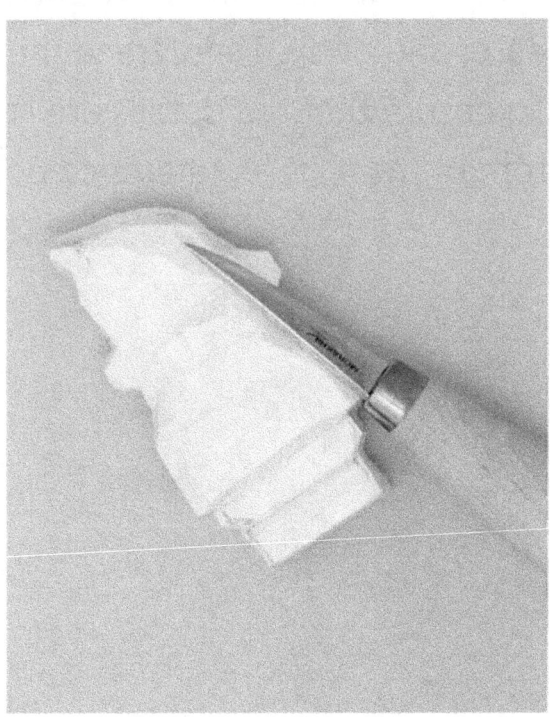

5. Shape the ears and shoulders. Use the push cut to round the sides of the face and plane the ears' front and back until they are about ¼ inch wide. Round the tops of the shoulders and the hard corners on the hat.

6. Trace the detail pattern. Cut the front-view pattern into four sections: hat, face, beard, and body. Then, trace the details onto the front of the gnome. To ensure that the details are lined up properly, use the ears and the bottom of the shirt as reference points.

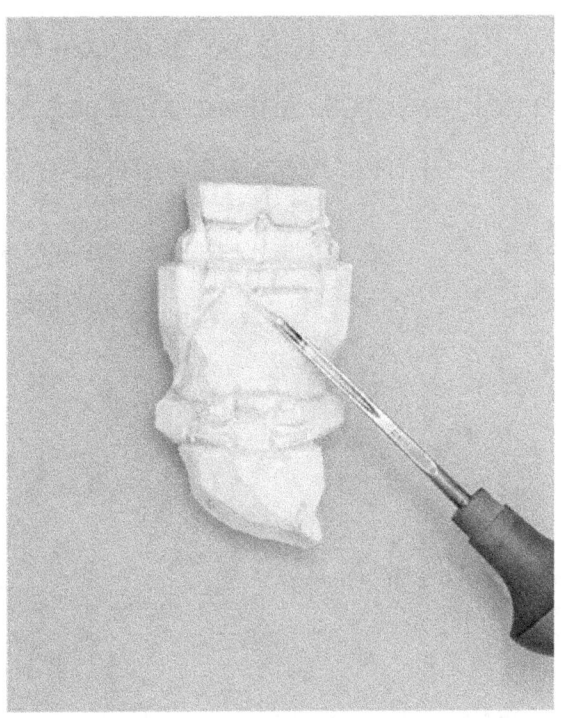

7. Carve the detail lines. Use the v-gouge to whittle the detail lines on the front of the gnome.

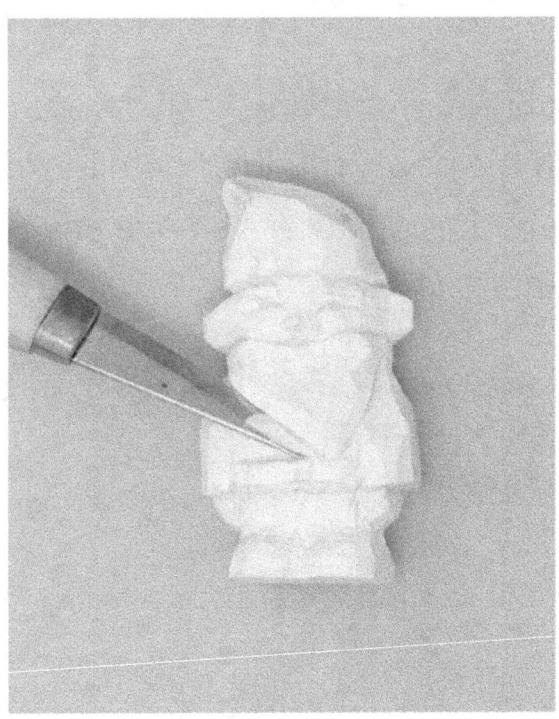

8. Shape to the detail lines. With the skew chisel or the tip of your knife, round the gnome's facial features. Shape the face toward the nose and eyebrows. Round the top of the beard toward the ears.

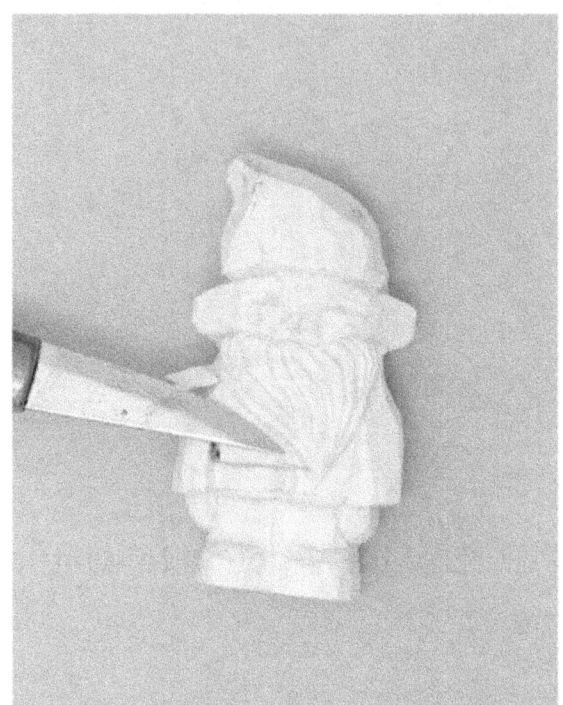

9. Clean up the details and round any hard edges. Use the v-gouge to clean up and sharpen the newly rounded details. Add wavy lines to the eyebrows and beard for hair texture. Remove any pencil marks and smooth any hard corners.

> **TECHNIQUE TIP:** If you display your gnome outside in the garden, be sure to coat it with a weather-resistant finish like polyurethane.

Chess Pieces

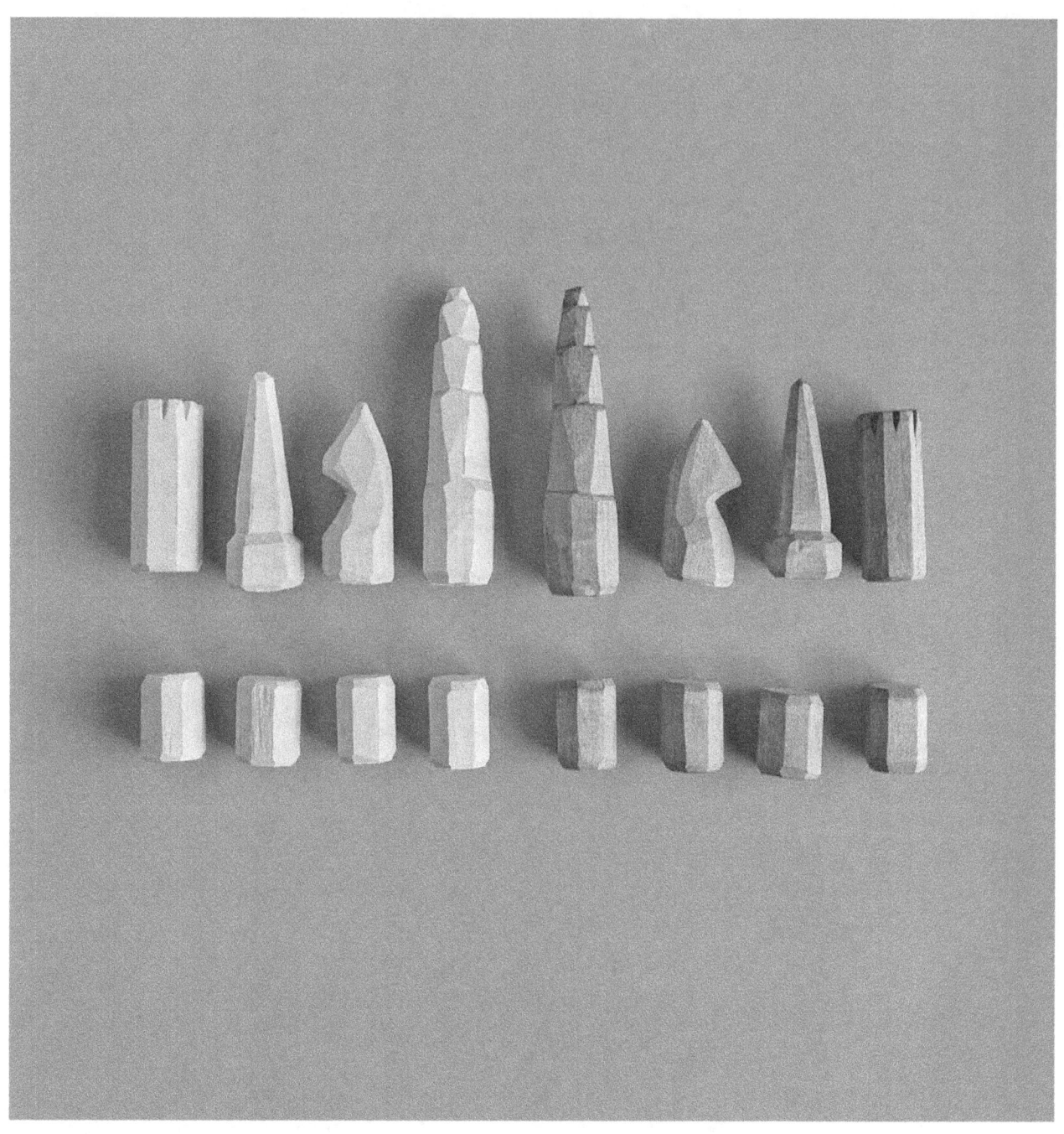

The 32 pieces of a chess set can take ages to whittle individually. But here, each type of piece in the set is whittled in a batch and then separated, saving you time and energy.

START-TO-FINISH TIME:

2 hours 30 minutes

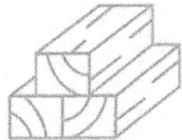

WOOD DIMENSIONS:

7 blocks of basswood measuring 1 inch square, four of which measure 8 inches long and three of which measure 10 inches, 6 inches, and 7 inches long

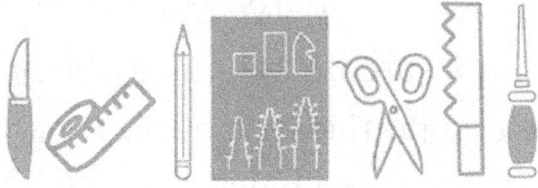

SUPPLIES:

Whittling knife, measuring tape, pencil, pattern, scissors, saw, detail gouge

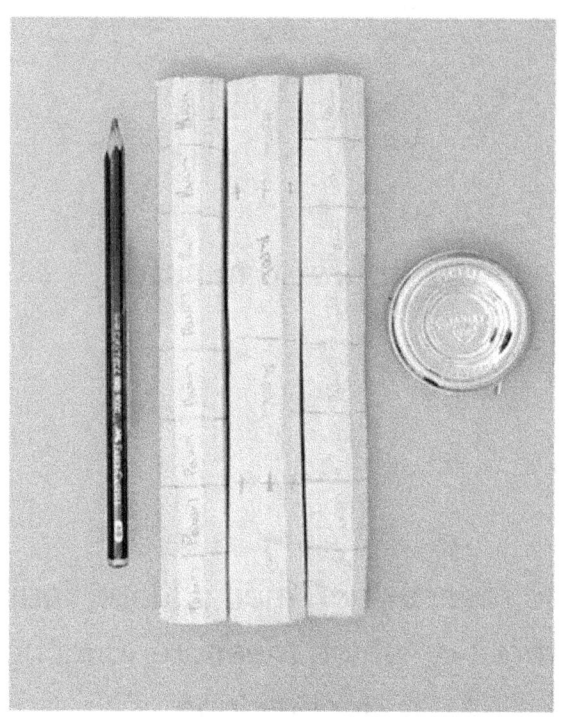

1. Whittle the rooks and pawns. Carve the vertical corners of three of the 8-inch blocks until they are octagonal (eight-sided) in cross-section. Draw a horizontal line around the stick every 2 inches on the rook block and every 1 inch on the two pawn blocks. Mark the turret lines on the center of each facet at the top of each rook.

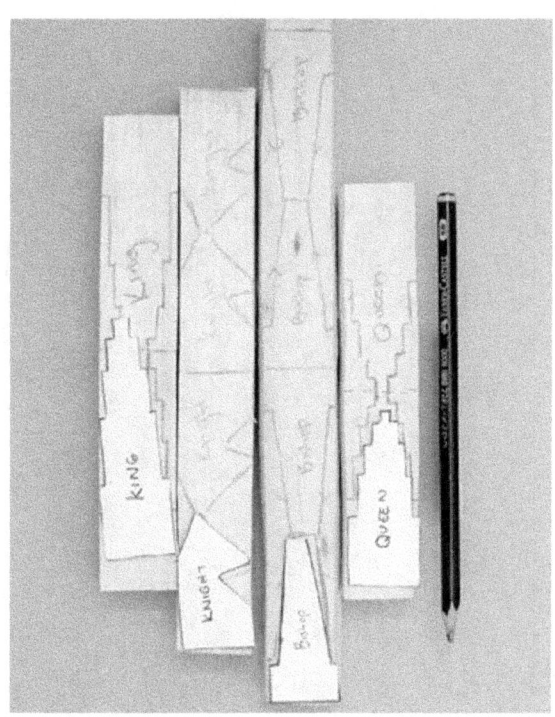

2. Transfer the patterns onto the remaining blocks. Cut out the patterns (you may want to copy them first and then cut them out). Trace the bishop pattern on the 10-inch block 4 times, the queen on the 6-inch block 2 times, the king on the 7-inch block 2 times, and the knight on the final 8-inch block 4 times. Repeat on the backside of each block, taking care to line up the patterns.

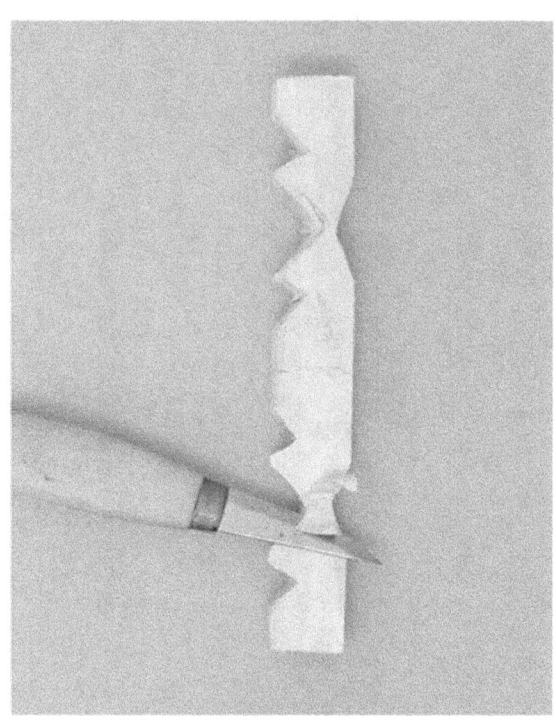

3. Whittle the knights. Use the v-cut to whittle the front and back profiles of each knight. Then, use a 2-sided push cut to taper the sides of each piece, beginning the cut at the top of each base. Continue until the heads are about ¼ inch thick.

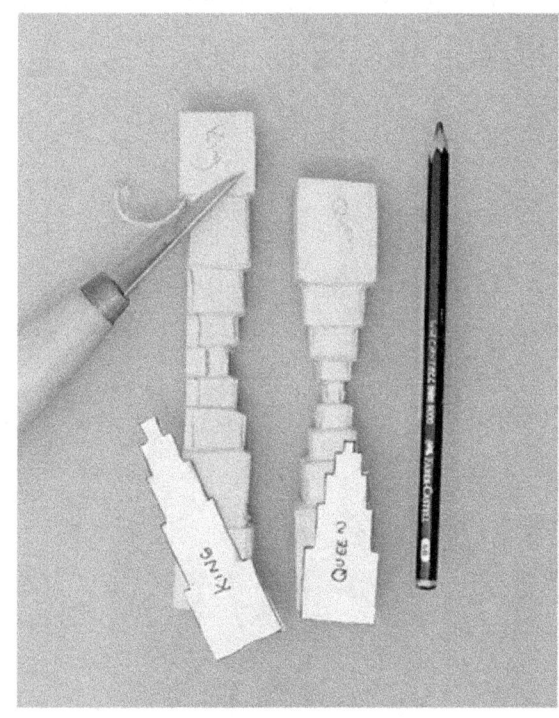

4. Carve the queens and kings. Use a series of stop cuts to whittle the side profiles of the king and queen blocks. Begin with the widest stop cuts to gradually thin the pieces as you go. Then, retrace the patterns on the newly carved faces and repeat on the front and back.

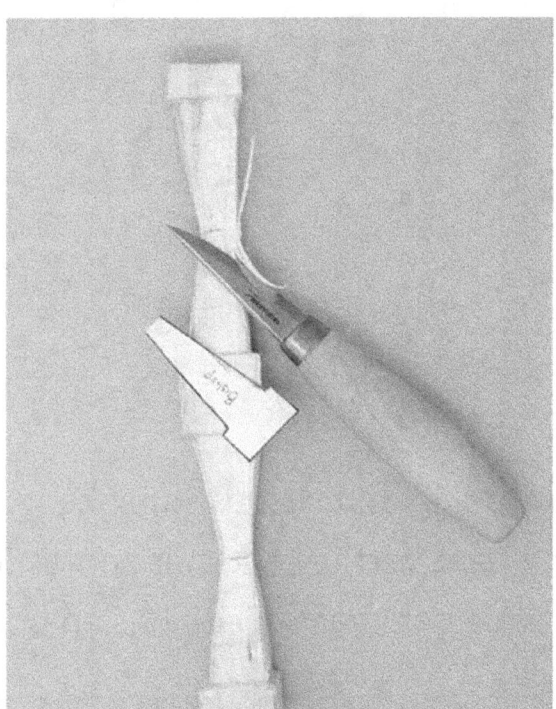

5. Shape the bishops. Use a stop cut to whittle the base of each bishop. Then, use a shallow v-cut to shape the tapered tops. Retrace the pattern on the newly shaped sides and whittle the front and back in the same way.

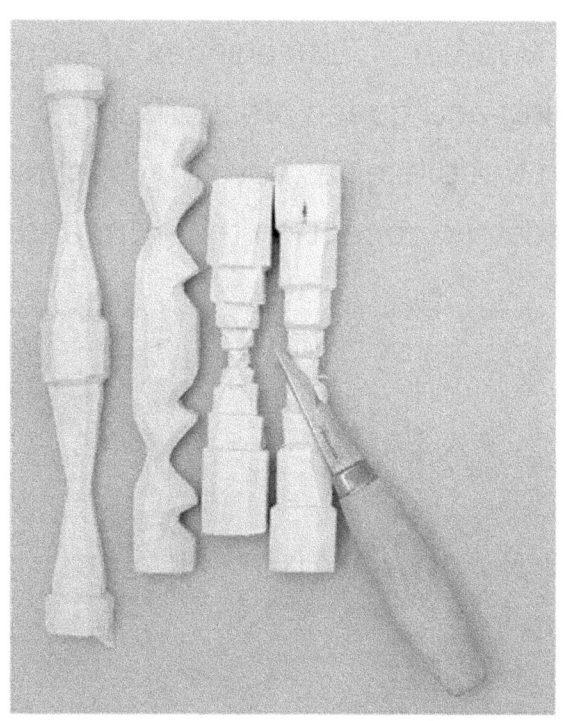

6. Round the corners of the knights, bishops, kings, and queens. Use a push cut to round any hard vertical and horizontal corners on the newly whittled pieces. Continue until each piece has an octagonal base.

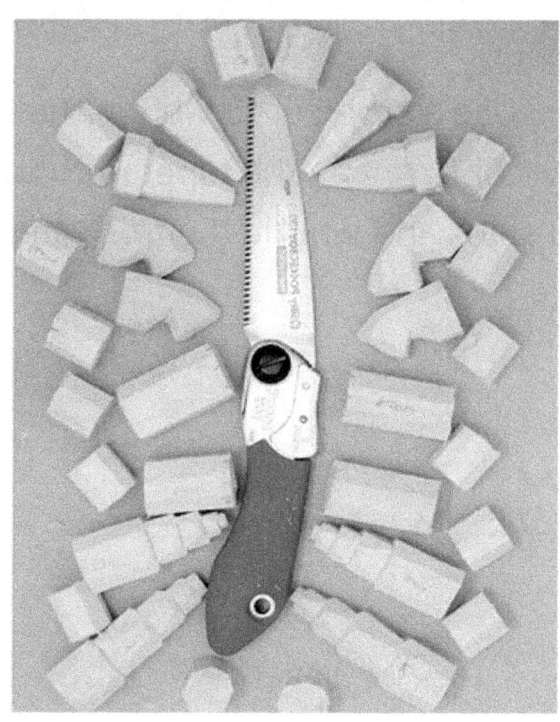

7. Separate each piece. Use the saw to separate each piece carefully. You should have sixteen pawns, four rooks, four knights, four bishops, two queens, and two kings. Clean up any saw marks with a controlled push cut.

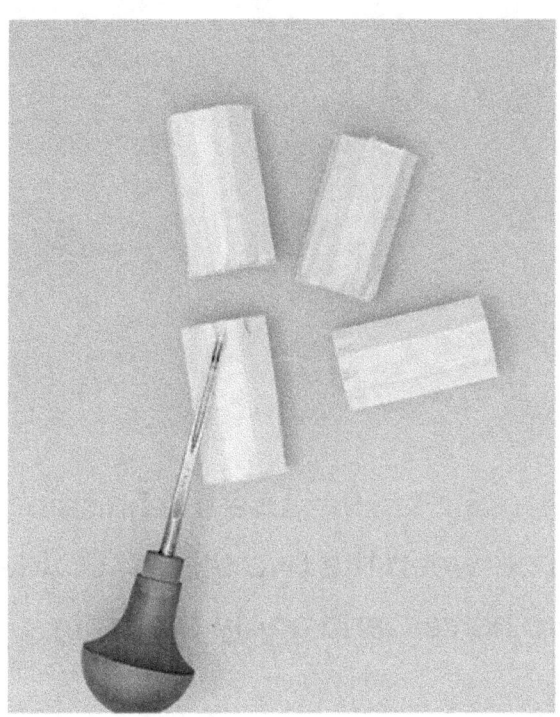

8. Whittle the details of the rooks. Use the smallest curved detail gouge to carve out the turret lines on the rooks.

9. Distinguish between the teams. Use the finishing technique of your choice to distinguish between the two teams. Divide the number of each type of piece into two halves, and apply the stain, paint, or varnish to one half.

> MIX IT UP TIP: This set is very geometric to make it beginner-friendly. Once you whittle this set, try making a set with more details and traditional shapes.

Wood Spirit

A wood spirit is a face carved into the side of a large stick to make it look like an ethereal guardian of the forest.

START TO FINISH TIME:
1 hour 15 minutes

WOOD DIMENSIONS:
A knot-free branch measuring 2 inches in diameter, and at least 6 inches long

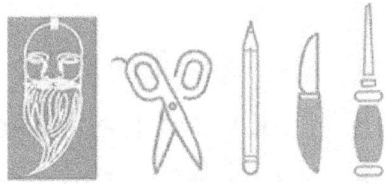

SUPPLIES:
Pattern, scissors, pencil, whittling knife, detail gouge

1. Trace the outline of the pattern. Cut out the pattern (you may want to copy it first and then cut it out) and trace the outer edges of the face and beard onto a knot-free section of the branch.

2. Shape the face area. Use a v-gouge to carve along the outer pencil lines. Use a skew chisel or the tip of your knife to carve the face and beard area smooth. Be sure to remove all bark within this space.

3. Draw the brow and nose. The brow and nose will be the high points on the face. Either carefully cut out and trace the brow and nose lines, or simply sketch them onto the face area.

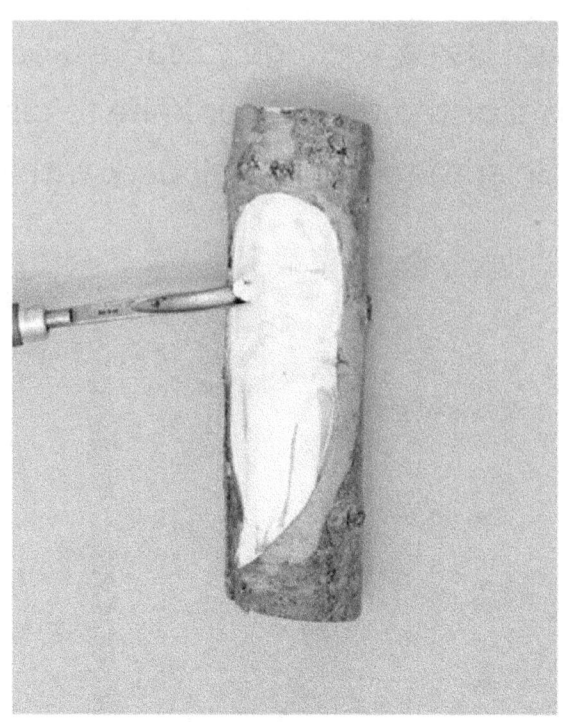

4. Whittle the general face shape. Use the curved detail gouge to hollow out the eye sockets and the sides of the nose. Use the stop cut to shape the horizontal intersection between the bottom of the nose and the moustache.

5. Transfer the details. Cut the pattern in half, using the top of the moustache as the dividing line. Carefully cut along the eye-detail lines. Transfer the details onto the face, taking care to center them and line up the edges.

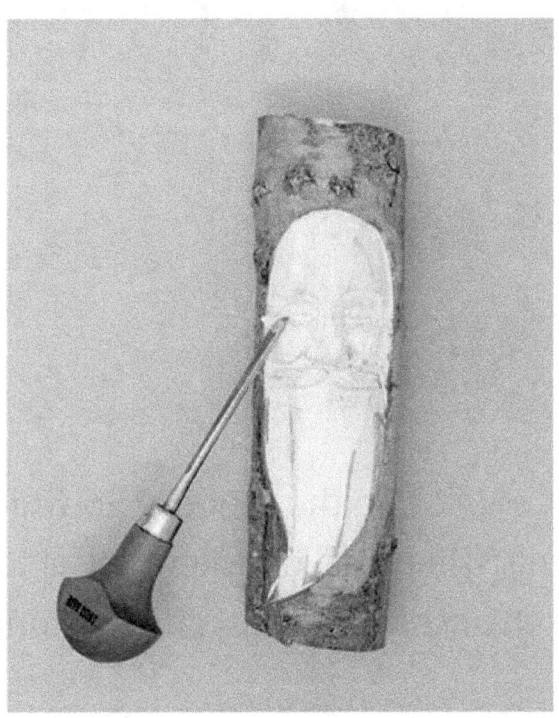

6. Shape the eye details. Use the v-gouge to whittle the eyelids and the closed-eye lines. Then, use the skew chisel to round the top and bottom eyelids as well as the brows and cheekbones.

7. Whittle the nose details. Use the v-gouge to whittle the lower lines of the nose and nostrils. Then, use the skew chisel to round the central nose ball. Repeat for the nostrils, making them slightly lower than the rest of the nose.

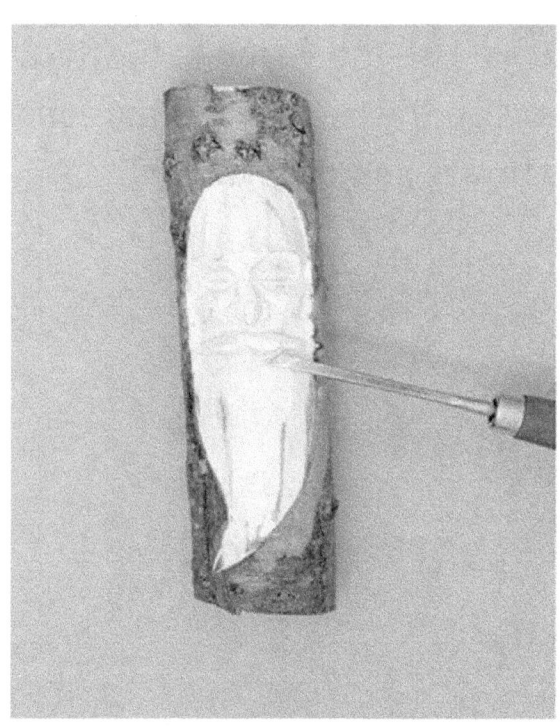

8. Carve the beard. First, carve the beard and moustache outlines with your v-gouge. Then, use the skew chisel or the tip of your knife to round the edges of the beard. Shape the beard so that it rounds down below the moustache.

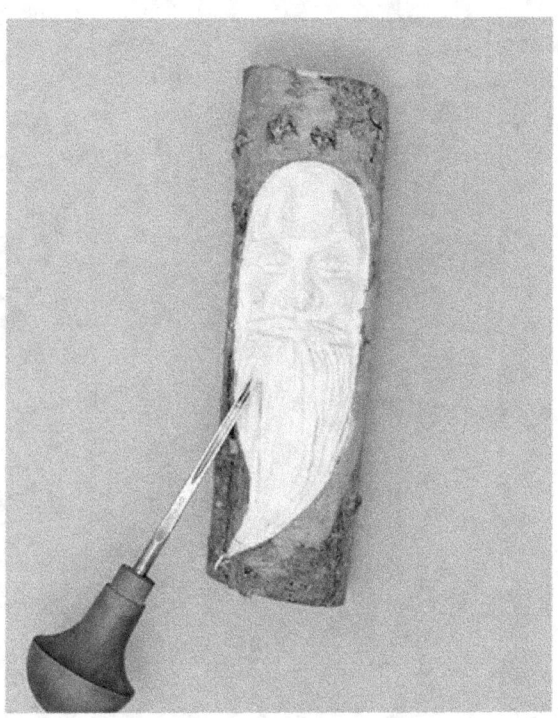

9. Add the hair texture and final details. Use the v-gouge to whittle horizontal hair texture into the moustache and eyebrows. Whittle vertical hair texture on the beard. Then, use the v-gouge to clean up and sharpen the details on the nose, eyes, and mouth.

> **PERSONALIZE IT TIP:** This project can also be whittled into the side of a walking stick. With some practice, you can alter the features to resemble someone you know.

PATTERNS

WHITTLED SPOON

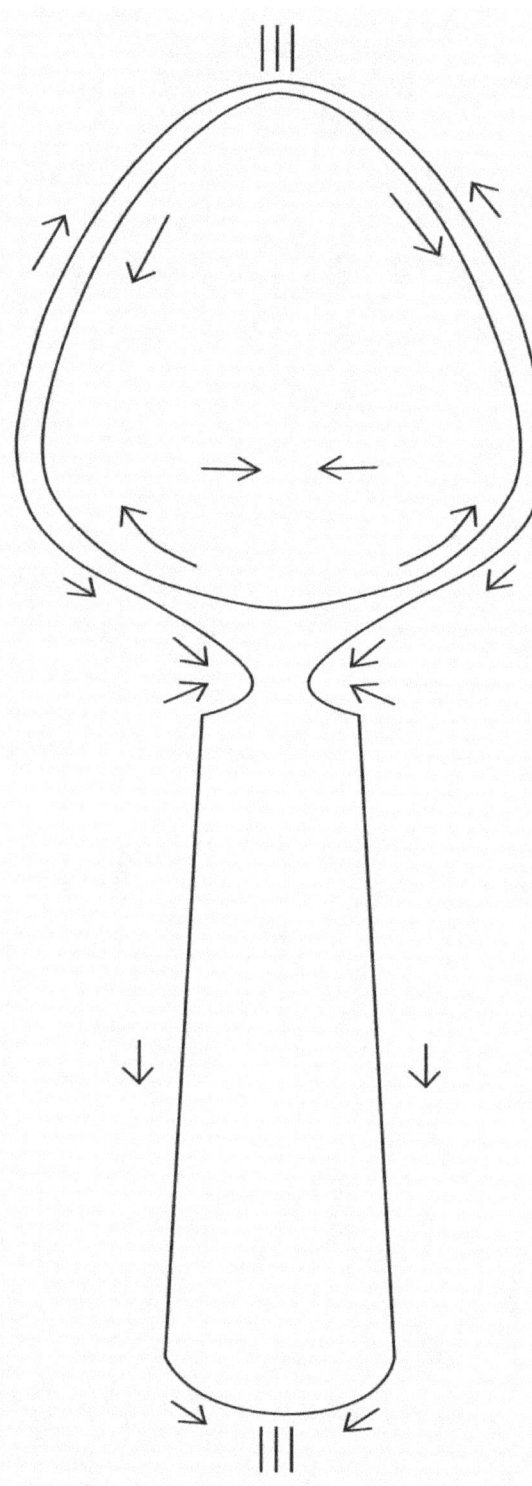

↓	**Carving direction**

Symbol	Meaning
‖‖‖	Grain orientation
– – –	Switch carving direction
↓	Straight cut
⇒	Push cut
⇗	V-shape cut
( ) ← ←	Ball cut
→ ⌐ ↑	Stop cut

FOX FIGURINE

TOP VIEW

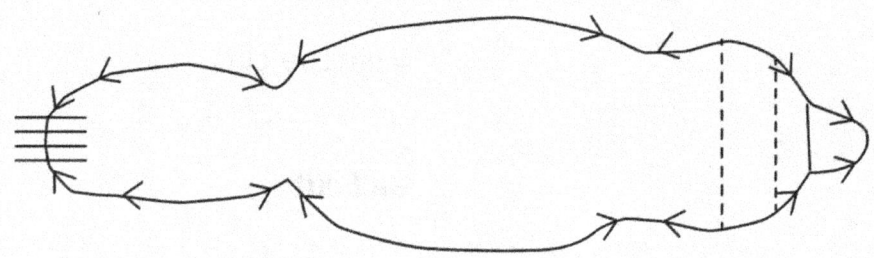

SIDE VIEW

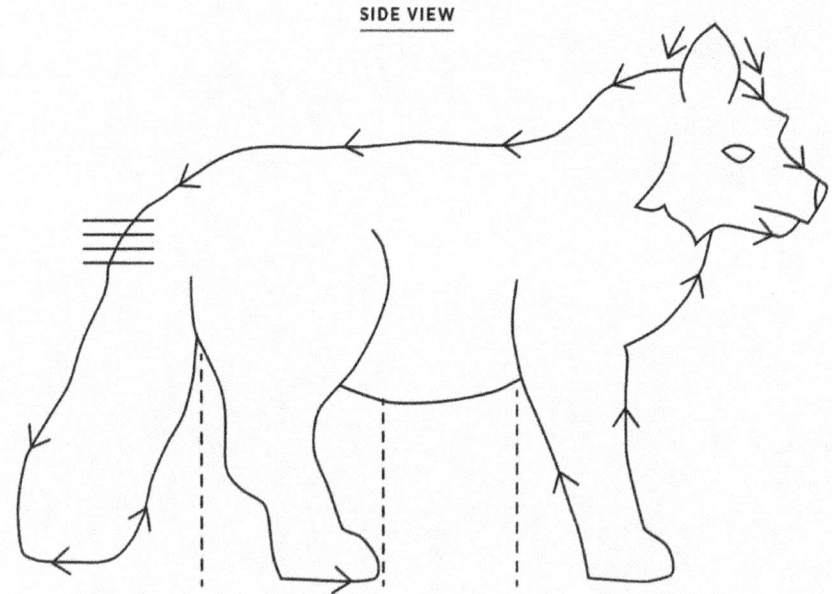

*See the **pattern key** for a reminder on how to interpret the pattern markers. Or refer to the project instructions.*

TOY BEAR

TOP VIEW

SIDE VIEW

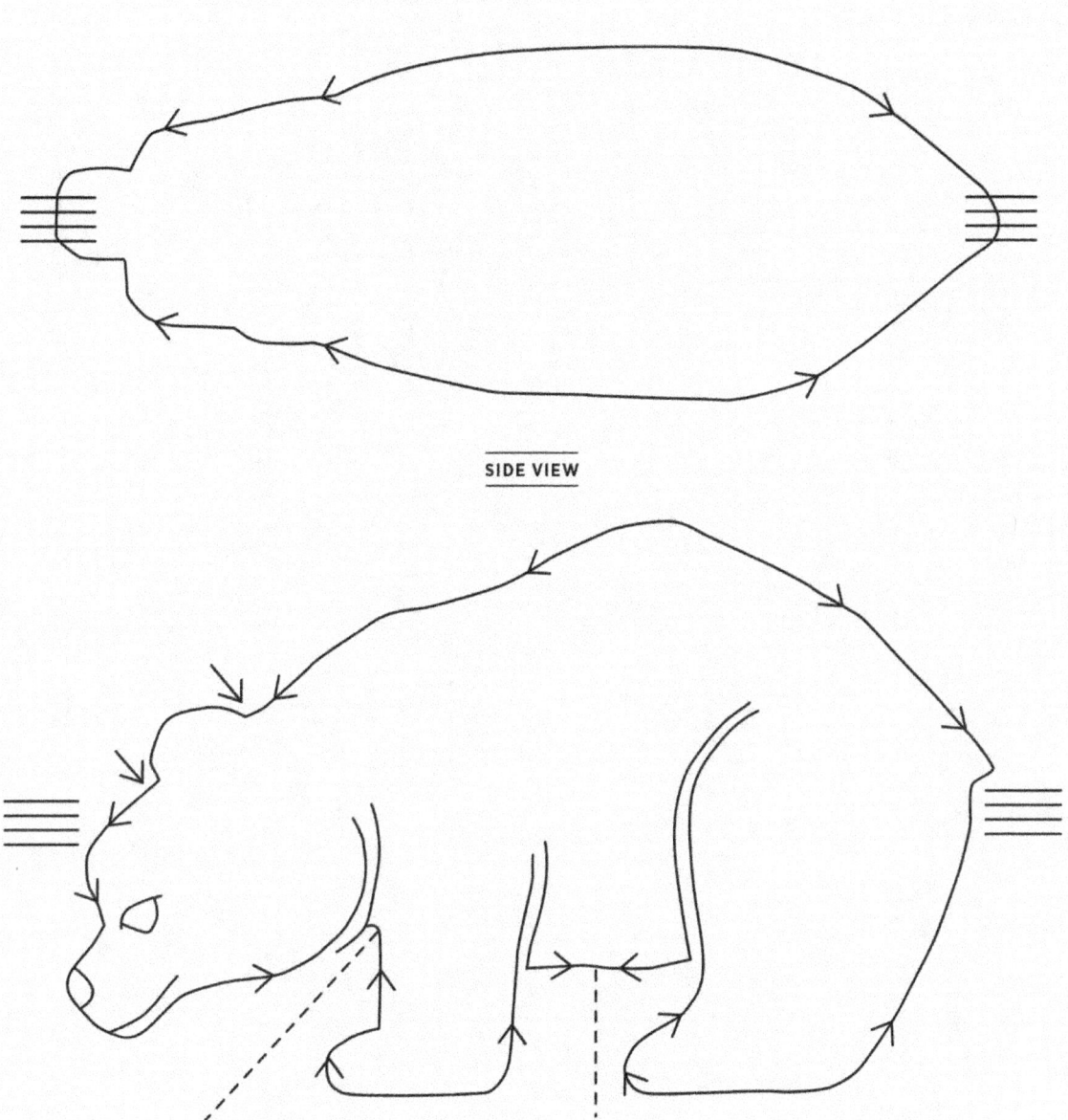

*See the **pattern key** for a reminder on how to interpret the pattern markers. Or refer to the project instructions.*

GARDEN GNOME

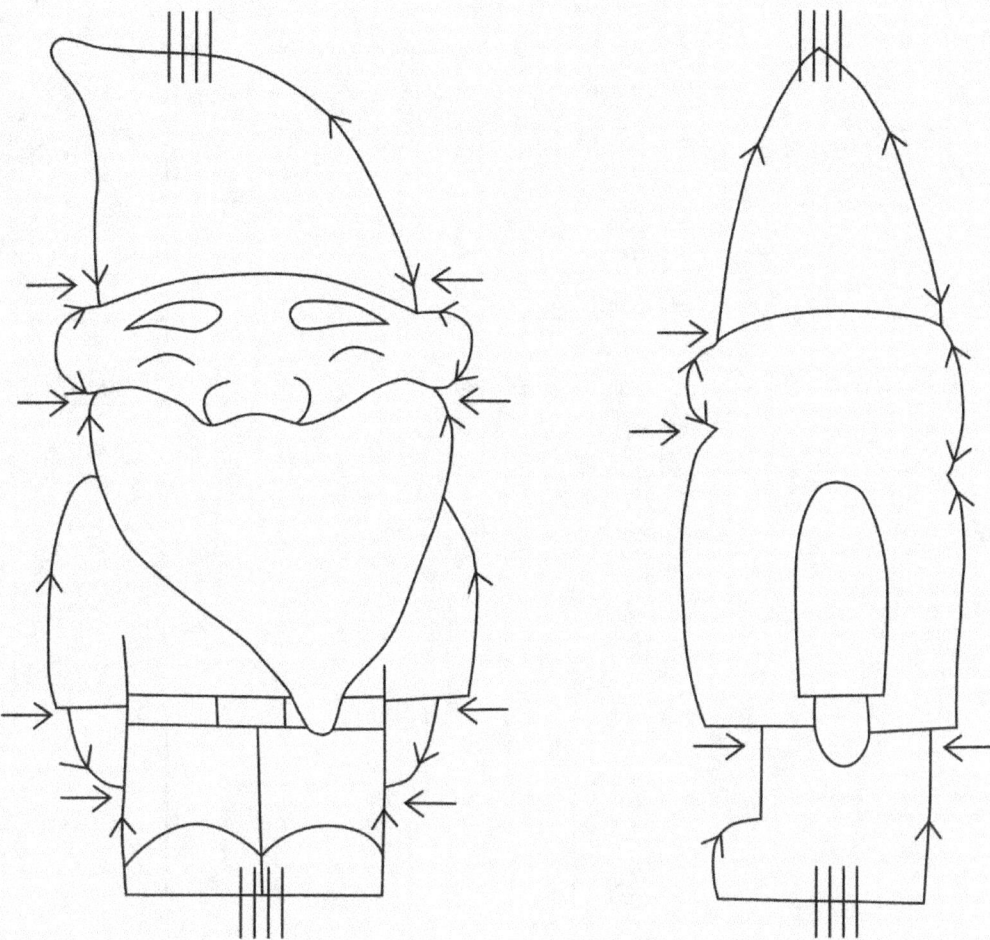

*See the **pattern key** for a reminder on how to interpret the pattern markers. Or refer to the project instructions.*

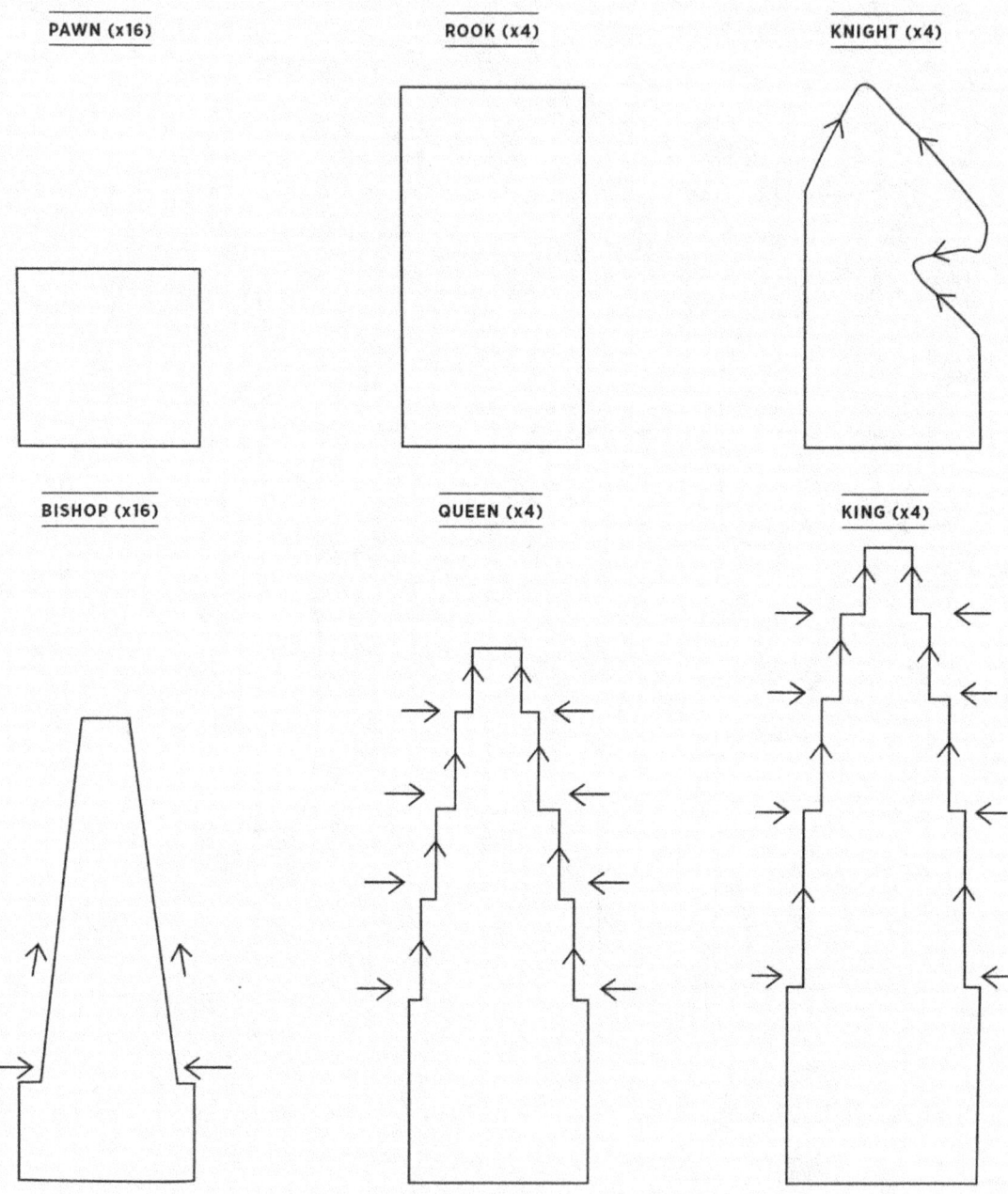

*See the **pattern key** for a reminder on how to interpret the pattern markers. Or refer to the project instructions.*

WOOD SPIRIT

FRONT VIEW

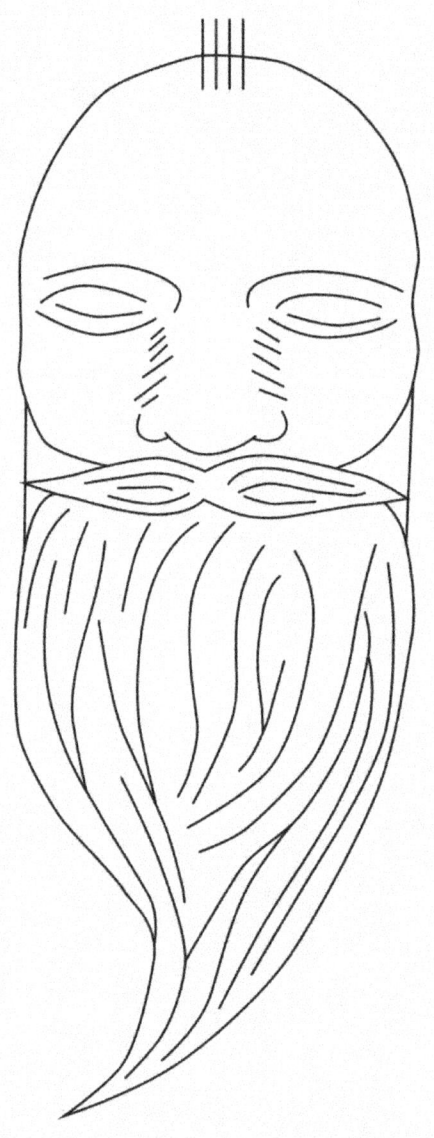

*See the **pattern key** for a reminder on how to interpret the pattern markers. Or refer to the project instructions.*

RESOURCES

Here are some trusted resources for tools, materials, knowledge, and community that will help you continue on your woodworking journey.

Websites

GARRETT WADE GarrettWade.com
Garrett Wade is a wonderful resource for tools, especially saws and detail gouges. A blog section contains many "how-to" articles.

LEE VALLEY TOOLS LeeValley.com
Lee Valley is a trusted resource for tools, especially for sharpening. It sells basswood blocks if you can't find any locally.

RAGWEED FORGE RagweedForgeStore.com
If you are looking for a place to buy your first whittling knife, try Ragweed Forge, which has one of the largest selections of and the lowest prices for Mora knives (a great beginner/intermediate knife).

RISE UP & CARVE RiseUpAndCarve.com
If you particularly enjoyed the wooden spoon project, you should look into Rise Up & Carve. This international community of whittlers and green woodworkers has a perpetual Zoom meeting. Anyone can log in and whittle with other woodworkers. A monthly "spoon template challenge" features a show-and-tell session.

WOODCARVING ILLUSTRATED WoodCarvingIllustrated.com

If you are looking for a magazine all about whittling, check out *Woodcarving Illustrated*. Each issue has "how-to" articles, tool reviews, and interviews with well-known whittlers.

WOODCRAFT Woodcraft.com

Woodcraft is a one-stop-shop for whittling wood and higher-end tools. It produces a well-known magazine with many projects and inspirational articles.

App

PICTURETHIS

If you want to find wood in the wild, you will likely need to identify it correctly. Plant identification apps have improved greatly over the years. PictureThis is very user-friendly and (according to a yearly Michigan State University study) delivers a correct identification more often than other identification apps. The free version of the app is all you need, so be sure to close out the premium version pop-up ads when you first download it. Although these apps are getting more accurate, they still average around a 60 to 70 percent correct identification, so be sure to check a few sources if the identification is important.

Social Media Groups

If you are looking for other woodworkers and whittlers, groups on social media can be a great resource. There are several great Facebook groups, including Spoon Carving, Green Woodworking and Sloyd, Whittling Club, and Whittling and Wood Carving. They are a great place to ask questions, share projects, and find inspiration.

Acknowledgments

Thank you to all my friends and family who have encouraged and supported me and put up with the increased quantity of woodchips and sawdust.

www.ingramcontent.com/pod-product-compliance
Lightning Source LLC
Chambersburg PA
CBHW081106080526
44587CB00021B/3472